Well-being Wins for Teachers

This exciting and inspiring text offers easy-to-implement strategies and tools to improve teacher well-being in schools. Teacher well-being is of paramount importance in the profession and has never been as necessary as it is today, even being included at the heart of the current Ofsted framework. Drawing together theory, popular culture and real-life stories from teachers, each chapter focuses on one of ten inspirational and iconic individuals from diverse backgrounds as archetypes to explore key strands of well-being including healthy habits, resourcefulness, resilience, managing pressure, workload, time management and positivity.

Emphasising the importance of well-being and aspiration for teachers at all stages of their career, the chapters feature:

▶ a constructed definition of each icon and how their achievements translate into the teaching profession

▶ a case study exploring how a teacher has overcome well-being challenges in their career and how this shaped them as a professional

▶ key lessons and takeaway actions.

Including a foreword by Hannah Wilson, Co-founder and Director of Diverse Educators, *Well-being Wins for Teachers* translates the abstract notion of well-being into tangible and practical strategies for all teachers.

Tracey Leese is an assistant headteacher, literacy and English specialist, ECF and ITE lead and writer. Tracey is an award-winning advocate for women and mother of two.

Charlotte Rowley is a primary headteacher with over ten years' experience teaching English and leading in secondary schools. She is passionate about empowering others and has extensive experience in supporting and mentoring trainees and early career teachers.

Lauren Brown is an illustrator, graphic designer and art director.

"In a recruitment and retention crisis, where teachers are struggling under the weight of expectations, well-being has never been more vital. But well-being can sometimes seem like an abstract concept and this honest book cuts through the fluff, offering real tangible tips, discussion points and case studies which will really make a difference. Not only is it realistic and pragmatic, it is also hilarious. Its links to pop culture make a sensitive, important topic come to life. It'll make a real difference to school staff and in turn, the children they serve."

— **Haili Hughes**, *Director of Education at IRIS Connect, Mentoring Lead at the University of Sunderland*

"Finally a book that looks at well-being beyond education and a book that looks at mental health and well-being through an intersectional lens"

— **Hannah Wilson**, *Co-founder and Director of 'Diverse Educators'*

Well-being Wins for Teachers

What We Can Learn from Iconic Individuals

Tracey Leese and Charlotte Rowley
Illustrated by Lauren Brown

LONDON AND NEW YORK

Designed cover image: Lauren Brown

First published 2024
by Routledge
4 Park Square, Milton Park, Abingdon, Oxon OX14 4RN

and by Routledge
605 Third Avenue, New York, NY 10158

Routledge is an imprint of the Taylor & Francis Group, an informa business

© 2024 Tracey Leese and Charlotte Rowley

The right of Tracey Leese and Charlotte Rowley to be identified as authors of this work has been asserted in accordance with sections 77 and 78 of the Copyright, Designs and Patents Act 1988.

All rights reserved. No part of this book may be reprinted or reproduced or utilised in any form or by any electronic, mechanical, or other means, now known or hereafter invented, including photocopying and recording, or in any information storage or retrieval system, without permission in writing from the publishers.

Trademark notice: Product or corporate names may be trademarks or registered trademarks, and are used only for identification and explanation without intent to infringe.

British Library Cataloguing-in-Publication Data
A catalogue record for this book is available from the British Library

ISBN: 978-1-032-52910-3 (hbk)
ISBN: 978-1-032-52911-0 (pbk)
ISBN: 978-1-003-40911-3 (ebk)

DOI: 10.4324/9781003409113

Typeset in Optima
by codeMantra

This book is dedicated to our families (Leeses, Barkers, Rowleys, Smiths, Pickerings, Browns and Nultys) without whom our careers – and of course this book – would not be possible. We would especially like to single out the children of these families – Jack and Ollie Leese, Noah Kliment, and Oliver and Penny Brown – those who stand to benefit most from the well-being wins afforded by this project.

With sincere and heartfelt thanks and gratitude to you all …

Tracey, Charlotte and Lauren.

Contents

Acknowledgements ix
About the Authors and Illustrator xi
Foreword by Hannah Wilson xiii

1	Let Them Eat Cake	1
2	Winning at Well-being	7
3	Well-being Win 1: Beyoncé and Healthy Habits	11
4	Well-being Win 2: Robbie Williams and Resourcefulness	21
5	Well-being Win 3: Dame Kelly Holmes and Resilience	31
6	Well-being Win 4: Stephen Hawking and Pressure	41
7	Well-being Win 5: Taylor Swift and Workload	51
8	Well-being Win 6: Marcus Rashford and Compassion	61
9	Well-being Win 7: Dolly Parton and Time Management	71
10	Well-being Win 8: Joe Wicks and Positivity	81
11	Well-being Win 9: Tina Turner and Self-awareness	91
12	Well-being Win 10: Tom Daley and Creativity	101
13	Conclusion	111

Afterword 115
Index 119

Acknowledgements

Well-being Wins for Teachers would not exist without *Teach Like a Queen*; therefore it would be remiss not to acknowledge the role that WomenEd and Christopher Barker indirectly played in this project.

Sincere thanks to Annamarie Kino and Sophie Ganesh and all the team at Routledge for their belief in this book – and all of their tireless work and support throughout the process.

Our classroom cases study icons are the true stars of the book. A huge thank you to Luke Dipple, Mark Rayner, Kiran Satti, Liz Todd, Sarah Beasley, Fiona Dutton, Victoria Brickley and of course to the other icons who didn't want to be named. We are so grateful that they shared their brilliance with us, so that we may share it with you.

Massive thanks to the legend that is Hannah Wilson for her incredible foreword for getting behind us and this project. Heartfelt thanks to Haili Hughes for her amazing endorsement too.

To Lauren Brown – the most incredible creative visionary who has created stunning illustrations which have captured the concept of winning at well-being perfectly.

Finally, a special thank you to our respective families – especially Jack and Ollie who have had to share their mum with the creation of a book (again!)

About the Authors and Illustrator

Tracey Leese BA (hons) MA PGCE FCCT is a secondary assistant headteacher, literacy and English specialist, ECF lead and writer. Tracey is an award-winning advocate for women and mother of two. Tracey's debut book *Teach Like a Queen* was published in 2022.

Charlotte Rowley BA (hons) LLB, MA, PGCE, FCCT is a primary school principal and foundation governor. She is passionate about empowering others and has extensive experience in supporting and mentoring trainees and early career teachers. Outside of work, she is a marathon runner, charity volunteer, reader, writer and poet from Stoke-on-Trent.

Lauren Brown BA (hons) is a graphic designer, illustrator, marketing expert and mother of two who attended the University of Salford. Lauren currently works as an art director and is a true creative with a passion for all things aesthetic, including interior design. Lauren illustrated *Teach Like a Queen* which was published in 2022.

Foreword

Hannah Wilson,
Co-founder and Director of Diverse Educators

Mental health and well-being (MHWB) are themes I have thought about, talked about and written about a lot in the two decades I spent in teaching. As a headteacher I ensured that we centred them as a priority, that we had the difficult conversations which led to us being the first school in our county to achieve the Gold Mental Health in Schools Award.

I passionately believe that if we look after our staff, they will look after our students. There is a reason why airlines instruct you to put on your own life jacket or secure your own oxygen mask first, as it gives you the best chance of being in the right shape to help others. The well-being of our students should not be at the expense of the well-being of our staff.

Since leaving the system and going independent as a leadership development consultant, coach and trainer, I have spent a lot of time supporting schools, colleges and trusts. My work on culture and ethos; coaching and mentoring; values and ethics; leadership; diversity, equity, inclusion and belonging all ultimately impact the mental health and well-being of all stakeholders. Thus, this book resonates with me and my vision, mission and values as it ties those threads together to create a tapestry.

Much has been published since the Secretary of State for Health and the Secretary of State for Education presented the Green Paper *Transforming Children and Young People's Mental Health Provision* to Parliament in December 2017. The MHWB market has become commercialised and at points saturated so we often hear the same repeated messages from the same voices. Moreover, the message is also delivered through a lens that centres white identities.

So, when I was asked to support the publication of another book, I was a bit cynical! Until I read the pitch – finally a book that looks at well-being beyond education and a book that looks at MHWB through an intersectional lens.

FOREWORD

As a sector we are clearly not getting staff well-being right. If we are really honest with ourselves, we are a sector in crisis. We struggle to recruit (and we struggle even more to retain) our school staff. Something has got to give and it should not be our human resource. The annual Teacher Well-being Index is a hard read. The 2023 report confirms that:

- 78% of teachers are stressed
- 55% of all school staff think their school culture negatively impacts their well-being
- 46% of all staff say their organisations do not support employees with MHWB problems
- 39% of all staff have experience a MHWB issue in the last year.

We have a lot of challenges to understand, to navigate and to resolve as we cannot continue to let the state of our staff's well-being deteriorate. If we keep doing the same, we will keep getting the same – we need to take stock and affect real lasting change. Hence, it is time for us to look beyond the sector for role models and examples of best practice.

Well-being Wins for Teachers is here to bring a different perspective to help us to look outwards to change the conversation. The book takes a holistic approach to teacher well-being, to make suggestions for a systemic approach to initiating, implementing and instituting change that has impact. Each chapter is pragmatic and practical with suggested strategies and tools that can be lifted to create change at an individual and a whole school level via 'stackable habits'. In each chapter there is an archetype, well-being wins, a case study, talking points and takeaways, which are all cross-referenced to the DfE's MHWB framework for schools. The authors' shared vision is to consider what a culture of mental health and well-being looks like and feels like for its staff stakeholders.

The cross-sector role models are a great way to humanise the behaviours we need to see in schools and the character attributes we need to embody to activate a culture of well-being. The archetypes are Beyoncé, Dolly Parton, Joe Wicks, Dame Kelly Holmes, Marcus Rashford, Robbie Williams, Professor Stephen Hawking, Taylor Swift, Tina Turner and Tom Daley– there really is someone for everyone. It reminds me of how schools often name their houses after living role models, and often identify Values Champions and Character Ambassadors who the learners can identify with. (If this is an approach you are taking or are considering taking in your own school with your pupils then do look at the great work of some of our partner organisations: Amazing People Schools, Human Values Foundation and Lyfta.)

The use of the archetype to personify values and behaviours made me think of John Kotter's *My Iceberg is Melting* allegory. If you have not read it, then I recommend it as a quick and entertaining read on change management; it is the story of a penguin colony and is set on an iceberg which is apt for climate justice conversations. Each way we can respond to change is characterised as a different penguin. *Well-being Wins for Teachers* takes a similar approach to bring to life the changes in perspective we need to manifest in our schools and across our system. Central to both texts is healthy dialogue and resourcefulness.

At the heart of change are communication and relationships. Effective change is sustained when we are aware of ourselves, of others and of our environment. If this book does one thing I hope it models inclusive representation and encourages us to consider well-being through the lens of each Protected Characteristic, as outlined in the Equality Act (2010).

My well-being archetype would be the late, great Maya Angelou. She is one of my favourite writers and poets, and it is she who inspired me to pursue post-colonial literature for my degree to then become an English teacher. Her character attributes of passion, compassion and resilience made her an empowered and inspiring individual. She is someone who navigated and processed a lot of trauma in her lifetime which relates to the Adverse Childhood Experiences as outlined by Dr Nadine Harris which a lot of UK schools now use as part of their well-being framework.

Her wisdom is captured in the following quotes:

My mission in life is not merely to survive, but to thrive; and to do so with some passion, some compassion, some humour, and some style.

Do the best you can until you know better. Then when you know better, do better.

I will leave you with two questions to consider as you read each chapter.

▶ How can we move our staff's well-being from survival mode to thriving mode?
▶ How can we learn from the archetypes and the case studies in this book to be better and to do better when it comes to our MHWB approaches in our schools, colleges and trusts?

References

EdSupport (2023) Teacher Wellbeing Index (October). Available at www.educationsupport.org.uk/resources/for-organisations/research/teacher-wellbeing-index/ (accessed 25 October 2023).

Kotter, J. (2016) *Our Iceberg is Melting*. Penguin Random House.

UK Government (2017) Transforming Children and Young People's Mental Health Provision to Parliament. Available at https://assets.publishing.service.gov.uk/media/

FOREWORD

5a823518e5274a2e87dc1b56/Transforming_children_and_young_people_s_mental_health_provision.pdf (accessed 25 October 2023).

UK Government (2023) Promoting and Supporting Mental Health and Well-being in Schools and Colleges. Available at www.gov.uk/guidance/mental-health-and-wellbeing-support-in-schools-and-colleges (accessed 25 October 2023).

Resources

Amazing People Schools: https://uk.amazingpeopleschools.com/
Human Values Foundation: https://humanvaluesfoundation.com/
Lyfta: www.lyfta.com/

INTRODUCTION

A Chapter by Tracey

Let Them Eat Cake

In this chapter we will explore key questions such as:

- What is well-being?
- Can I have my (figurative) cake and eat it?
- Can I have my (literal) cake and eat it?

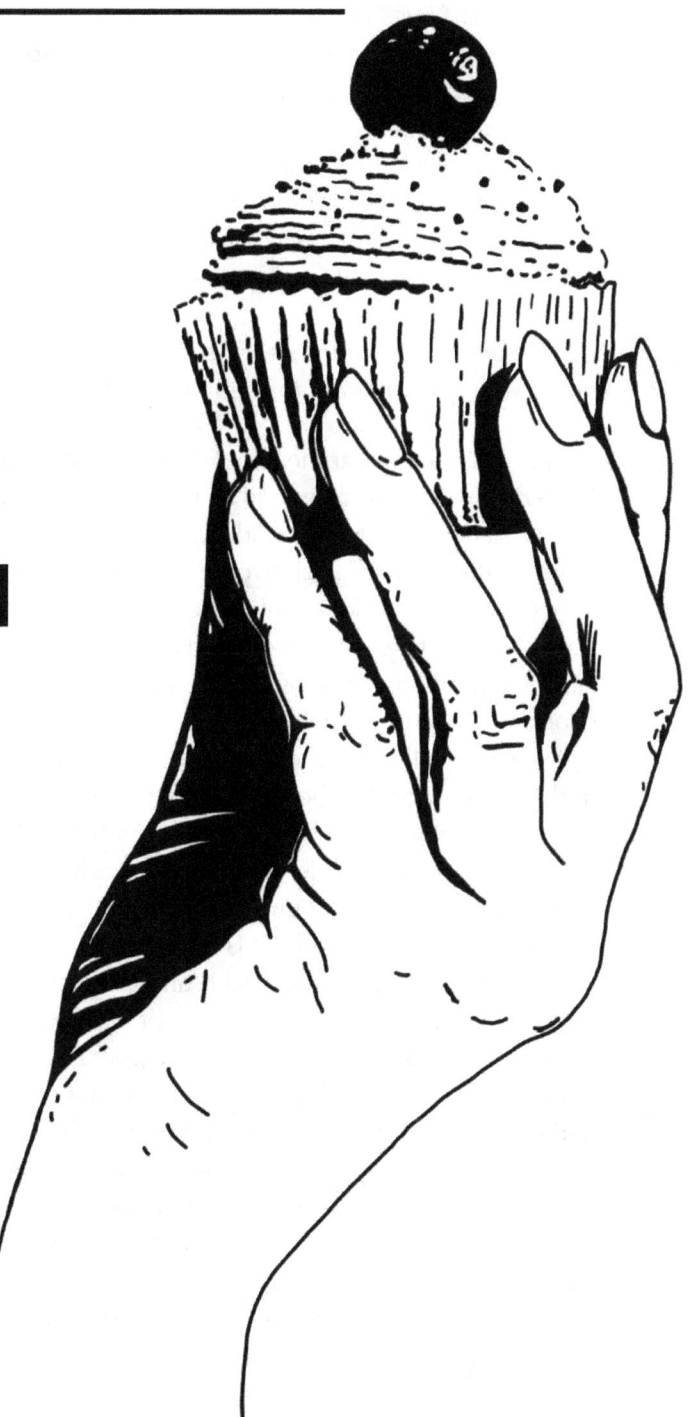

It's Monday morning and Mina has spent Sunday afternoon marking thirty Year 11 essays – then adapted her curriculum sequence to respond to whole-class misconceptions. Though Mina gets to school at 7:30am, the photocopier is broken and she arrives at whole-staff briefing with no time to spare. The teacher of her parallel set has rung in sick and she has been asked to send a cover lesson to her head of department because the colleague was too unwell to do this. By break time Mina has fifteen emails to respond to and doesn't make it out of her classroom. Mina teaches the rest of the morning, runs a chess club at lunch and teaches the final period before responding to additional emails.

At the end of the day, a dehydrated, starving Mina heads to a one-hour CPD session on staff well-being; she leaves with the action to audit her well-being and submit an evaluation by Friday, before heading home to plan and mark for the four lessons she has tomorrow.

Despite an attempt from the school to address issues of well-being, clearly there is more work to do in order to keep Mina in the profession until she retires.

In April 2023 the Department for Education published the *Working Lives of Teachers and Leaders* report: the findings and analysis of surveys with 11,177 teachers and over 9,000 school leaders about their workload and working practices. The findings of the report indicate that the average classroom-based full-time teacher works an average 51.9 hours a week, amid a backdrop of 'acceptable' workload and woefully low reports of job satisfaction and perceived workload autonomy.[1] Furthermore, in the *Teacher Well-being at Work* report published by TES in 2019, workload was cited as a key reason why staff choose to leave the profession.[2]

Teacher well-being is of paramount importance within the profession; we are in the midst of a national teacher recruitment crisis, which surely cannot continue unabated. Such is the onus placed on teacher well-being, it is now at the heart of the current Ofsted framework.[3] While this may not yet have revolutionised the widespread workload issue – the intent around long-term teacher well-being is clear – it has never been as important or necessary as it is today.

According to the UK's Health and Safety Executive, teaching staff and education professionals report the highest rates of work-related stress, depression and anxiety in Britain.[4] The *TES School Well-being Report 2023: UK* seeks to 'shine(s) a light on the ongoing tug-of-war of the teaching profession: while systemic issues such as funding and workload are continuing to push staff to their limit and even consider a move away from schools entirely in some cases the profession'.[5] It concludes that resourcing and workload are key issues affecting staff well-being. As teachers, this is neither new nor news: we are aware of the scarcity of time and capacity, but remain committed to delivering the best quality education for our students regardless.

Whilst the profession surely demands a more systemic approach to safeguard teachers' well-being, there is also a need to empower and equip teachers with strategies and tools to address this on an individual-practitioner level. This book is written with this aim in mind: to present the pursuit of well-being as something which is inherently possible through a series of small-scale wins – wins which can be implemented on an individual, department or whole-school level.

Though teacher well-being is heading towards crisis point, it feels important to remain resolutely solution focused in our response. By placing the potential for well-being wins into the hands of classroom practitioners and school leaders, it is our hope that teachers will feel empowered enough to influence the influenceable, control the controllable and place well-being back into the hands of teachers.

Representation of teachers in the media can feel like click bait and with so many aspects of the profession feeling weaponised as political pawns, it feels important to remind ourselves (and anyone else who needs to hear it) that teaching is the most glorious, rewarding and worthwhile profession in the world – and the stakeholders who really matter amid this are the children. Of course, one of the best ways to support children (who are experiencing their own well-documented well-being crisis) is by virtue of the adults they work with. Staff who are energised, resourced and well enough to navigate obstacles with smiles on their faces, modelling resilience is the very thing which could impact most positively on our learners' own mental health and well-being. However, we also need teachers to be able to function at this level with minimal cost to their personal well-being.

Well-being for teachers matters because:

- ▶ the mental and physical wellness of teachers directly correlates to the quality of education children receive
- ▶ teachers are role models for young people – if we demonstrably keep ourselves well this will empower those we teach to do the same
- ▶ teacher absence is costly and detrimental to colleagues, students and school culture.

Teacher well-being benefits teachers, students and schools directly – but also has further reaching implications to impact much more widely than specific schools and trusts.

Having Our Cake and Eating It

It feels important to note that what constitutes well-being is not homogeneous – for some it is a slice of cake and a non-work-based conversation in the staff room, for others it's time away from enforced interaction with their colleagues! There seems to be genuine confusion around what well-being is across the profession, because it differs so much from context to context. It is our hope that well-being can be seen not as a 'one size fits all' bolt-on, but rather as a key strand which runs through policy, school leadership and impact measures. While many schools seem to favour cake as a well-being strategy – granted many of us wouldn't say no to this – it's worth remembering that for others it could be a well-being trigger. It's important to think broadly and holistically about well-being because it is much more than cake and caffeine.

For me, well-being is a symptom of the culture and ethos within a given school – of course external directives will influence this – but the absence of the Sunday night sinking feeling and the knowledge that you will not be demonised if you're too unwell for school or make a mistake are all working litmus tests of the extent to which the culture and ethos in any given school is conducive to staff well-being. That isn't to say that a toxic school which promotes workplace martyrdom and unhealthy working practices yet offers free cake and yoga can deem that staff well-being has been addressed – because a school which is dedicated to its staff *being well* starts at decision- and policy-making level.

So though the profession has a long way to go, as teachers, leaders and stakeholders in education, it is our hope that we can reclaim well-being so that it is more than something which is done to us (or even for and with us) but something we can influence and own. Hence the title 'Well-being Wins': this is a phrase (that as far as I know) I have coined – it is now used within my own school – and a term we use within the Senior Leadership Team (SLT) which has come to drive many of the conversations around expectations and whole-school initiatives (even in the writing of the School Improvement Plan!) How can we chase the well-being wins? Even though we know that we can't solve the huge teacher well-being and workload crisis, we can at least mitigate against this as much as possible within our school and daily practice.

What Can We Learn From Iconic Individuals?

Each chapter will focus on one key strand of well-being which has been adapted by the Department for Education as a framework conducive to teacher well-being. We have aligned each chapter with an *iconic individual* who shows the well-being wins in action – these individuals will serve as archetypes from whom we have gleaned three well-being wins in their own words. It also feels important to point out that these influential figures are not affiliated with this project; we just admire them and we are offering them as inspiration of well-being in action. Clearly they are not teachers in the literal sense, so in order to contextualise the wins we have included a case study from a serving practitioner to help us take the inspiration from the global stage into our classrooms, schools and trusts.

You may also recognise that many of our iconic individuals have protected characteristics and so serve as positive representations of disability, ethnicity and gender – and are of course so much more than that too. This is a deliberate choice because in the same way that the profession needs to respond to the nationwide well-being challenges, there is also so much work to do in order to build more diversity within the profession at all levels – especially within leadership. Representation is a precursor to wider inclusivity and something we can all contribute towards as stakeholders.

It is our sincere hope that this book will arm you with practical strategies to help well-being feel winnable, and celebrate the achievements of iconic individuals while marvelling at our case study icons too. In short: chase the wins and ultimately well-being will follow …

Questions to Consider

- What metric can we use to measure well-being?
- Where can I make marginal gains in my school for staff well-being?
- How is well-being made a priority in my school?
- What common barriers are there to well-being – and what strategies can be put in place to remedy?
- What are the direct and indirect consequences of placing staff well-being at the heart of policy-making in schools?
- How can we take more responsibility for safeguarding our staff?

Notes

1. Department for Education (2023) Working Lives of Teachers and Leaders Wave 1. Available at www.gov.uk/government/publications/working-lives-of-teachers-and-leaders-wave-1 (accessed 4 November 2023).
2. TES (2022) TES Well-being Report. Available at www.tes.com/en-gb/for-schools/content/tes-wellbeing-report (accessed 31 August 2023).
3. Ofsted (2023) Education Inspection Framework. Available at: www.gov.uk/government/publications/education-inspection-framework/education-inspection-framework-for-september-2023 (accessed 31 August 2023).
4. Health and Safety Executive (2018) Work Related Stress, Depression or Anxiety Statistics in Great Britain. Available at: www.hse.gov.uk/statistics/ (accessed 31 August 2023).
5. TES, Well-being Report.

PREFACE

A Chapter by Charlotte

Winning at Well-being

In this chapter we will begin to explore how an intangibly complicated idea such as well-being can be broken down into a series of smaller wins and allow ourselves to imagine what those wins might amount to as part of a larger movement.

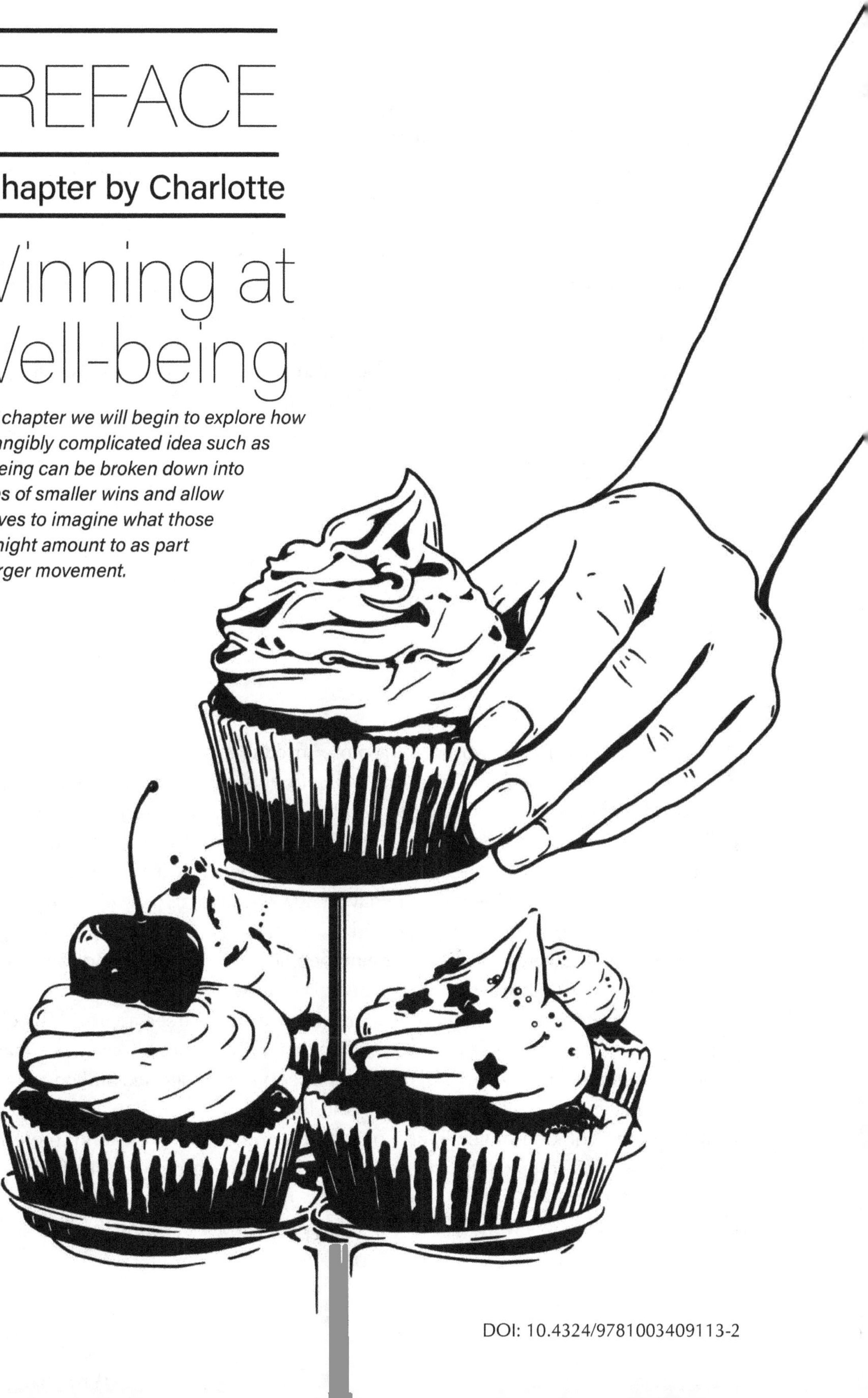

DOI: 10.4324/9781003409113-2

What Can This Book Offer You?

Aimed at anyone who works in a school, no matter what their role or experience, this book will shape practice and inspire. We make no promise to resolve *all* issues and take away the challenges immersed within education and we also recognise that well-being demands and requests can be bespoke and individual to specific settings. Thus, we appreciate that what works for some may not work for others. We do endeavour to share our own experiences and ideas that help with well-being and how the small wins may actually lead to larger victories, such as the power of managing workload, utilising time effectively, working smartly, changing our mindset to become more positive and, overall, gaining perspective and remaining energised and enthused in a profession that can be hugely impactful and joyful. Let's bring back that joy!

A range of well-known stars, past and present, are used as a foundation for each chapter, with these diverse icons and celebrity names linked to a particular trait. This book discusses their background, their successes and lessons that we can lift from them which may help with our own well-being. The overall intent is that as well as learning about their fame and achievements, we discover what serious lessons and 'wins' we can take away and transfer to our own practice.

Where Are We at With Well-being?

Well-being is a term that is used a lot more in education – and thank goodness for this! It is no longer unusual to have well-being forums or well-being discussion groups embedded within schools – in fact, this is daily practice. We cheer for the well-being policies embedded, are thankful for the well-being CPD and training, for the investment in care packages for colleagues and overall, are grateful that it is now acceptable for school leaders and Ofsted inspectors to have a new found focus for well-being, ensuring that unnecessary workload is not accepted or normalised.[1] These are all positive moves and show a shift towards individuals being happier, more content and, overall, more productive at work because a greater balance is restored.

In the current climate we have started to see a much freer approach to discussing mental health, well-being and work–life balance. These are all key areas that were barely even muttered a few years ago, let alone seriously recognised and considered for any kind of agenda. I am thankful for this and like many leaders I am passionate about recruiting the right kind of generation of teachers and educationists and, more importantly, *retaining* good teachers. The statistic of '1 in 4 teachers being likely to quit'[2] in certain areas is startling, yet the reported reality. Something needs to change, but also be *sustained* within this wonderful profession. This includes ensuring that it is no longer frowned upon to take well-being seriously nor deemed unusual to take time for *us*. Recuperating, resting and gaining perspective on priorities are vital to becoming better and well-rounded practitioners, whatever our role in school may be.

The term 'well-being', however, can be overcomplicated at times. Individuals, particularly leaders, may despair at the thought of having to be overly creative and original, perhaps ironically, their own well-being may be compromised because of thoughts of organising elaborate events, the expenditure of staff treats or creative initiatives all in the name of well-being balance in the workplace. It is possible for this intangibly complicated idea to be broken down into a series of smaller wins and allow ourselves to imagine what those wins might amount to as part of a larger movement, a well-being movement.

So How Can You Use This Book?

The main aim is that you delve into this book, learn some things that you perhaps did not know before and, most of all, have a new found realisation that it is often the little things that make a big difference to our mental health. The goal is that well-being is restored after finishing this, lessons are learned or, perhaps even more powerfully, you can teach others some of the 'wins' that we elaborate on, disseminating the information effectively in the form of light-hearted professional development for a range of educational teams all over the land.

We invite you to read the book from cover to cover (tell your friends about it!), but then hand-pick and revisit the chapters that really do 'speak to you'. At different times in the academic year, we may need reminders about various concepts.

- ▶ We may need more help at a certain point with time management and how to work smartly (turn to Dolly Parton for advice on this).
- ▶ Perhaps you need further assistance with positivity and transforming your mindset (please see Joe Wicks and how we can channel his energy into our own practice).
- ▶ Maybe we need to work on our resilience a little and need some actions and take-aways on how to build on this (turn to Dame Kelly Holmes for sound, poised advice).
- ▶ It might be time to remind ourselves of why we do what we do and how compassion is the basis of everything (Marcus Rashford will help with this one).

The truth is, we all need time to pause a little and reflect on our practice and, more importantly, what really counts. If we are not present, maybe find that our minds are just too full or feel 'out of sorts', I can guarantee that this book will add a little clarity and reassurance. Above all else, it reminds every one of us that we should be in this profession for the same reasons and should share the same goals – to support, teach, nurture and grow the next generation of pupils, but also the next generation of *colleagues* too. If we can normalise talking about our feelings and tangible actions and methods in which we can become more well-rounded educationists, teachers and leaders, just imagine the difference that we can make. Let's allow optimism in, restore calmness and solidify what is the best profession in the world!

Notes

1 Ofsted (2023) Education Inspection Framework. Available at www.gov.uk/government/publications/education-inspection-framework/education-inspection-framework-for-september-2023 (accessed 31 August 2023).
2 Martin, M. (2023) 1 in 4 Teachers Likely to Quit in 5 Years in Challenging Areas. TES, 6 June 2023. Available at: www.tes.com/magazine/news/general/teacher-retention-1–4-teachers-likely-quit-5-years-challenging-areas (accessed 10 November 2023).

WELL-BEING WIN 1

A Chapter by Tracey

Beyoncé and Healthy Habits

[verb] Reaching optimum efficacy through small consistent acts.

"In order to make it through term one I am going to have to Beyoncé my way through autumn."

To Do List:

Speaking as a millennial, it's hard to imagine a time pre-Beyoncé – when we weren't Crazy in Love, all (the) Single Ladies and prolific consumers of Lemonade. Such is the extent of Beyoncé's body of work that her name has evolved into a no-context-needed synonym for strength, performance and efficacy – to the extent where her surname is almost entirely superfluous.

Long before she was a mononymous icon, Beyoncé was born in Houston, Texas. It is well known that Beyoncé began her music career aged nine with the backing of her parents who both directed their respective skill-sets to her eventual success. Showing unwavering belief in his daughter, Matthew Knowles gave up his high-paid corporate role in order to manage the group Girl's Tyme – a platform from which Beyoncé and Kelly Rowland were able to hone their skills as performers. With Beyoncé's parents in their corner – Matthew as manager and Tina (her mother) as stylist – the group gained momentum and subsequently evolved into Destiny's Child, who after a series of line-up changes settled as a trio in the early 2000s and made history by receiving fourteen Grammys and selling more than sixty million records worldwide.[1]

For most artists this seismic career would be enough to dine off indefinitely, but this was a mere amuse-bouche in the case of Beyoncé whose behemoth, bar-raising solo career would go on to easily eclipse the girl group years. Beyoncé's solo sound – characterised by innovative production, off-the-scale vocals and empowering lyrics – would come to define (at least) a generation. From performing at the Superbowl to voicing a Disney character, Beyoncé's star has risen beyond all belief, and we get the sense that after decades in the industry, somehow she still hasn't peaked.

Uniting (in both music and matrimony) with Jay-Z boosted the profile of Queen Bey further, and his multiple alleged infidelities served as the muse for an entire concept album – from which Beyoncé emerged not as victim but victor, savagely hanging her husband out to dry (with a baseball bat in her hand no less) and ending years of press speculation in the process. Mic drop.[2]

In 2011 Beyoncé parted company with her father as her manager, challenging the patriarchy in the most literal way possible, enabling Beyoncé to flex more creative autonomy in the subsequent years. Like many of the icons we will come to discuss in this book, Beyoncé isn't afraid to own, and wield, her own power, not least of all because she has worked so hard to obtain it. She acts with intent and is an absolute master of her craft. Beyoncé is also widely considered to be a disruptor for challenging the status quo as a self-aware powerful black female artist.

Destiny's (Brain)Child

Essentially a child star, Beyoncé has avoided the fate which sadly befalls so many who sacrifice their childhood for careers – and outwardly at least appears to be both incredibly successful and well. As a mother of three, Beyoncé is fiercely protective of her family unit. We get the sense that in and amongst the career highs and undeniable success, Beyoncé's priorities and perspective are the very kind we need more of in our own fast-past (though infinitely less glamorous) profession.

While there is so much to admire about Beyoncé, we are going to focus mostly on the longevity she has cultivated in an industry which thrives on ephemeral success. Beyoncé has withstood so much in her multiple-decade career: where some artists work to constantly reinvent themselves as a response to emerging trends, Beyoncé's success feels much more organic and evolutionary. How can we as teachers command some of Beyoncé's tenacity without *breaking our souls* in the process?

Win 1: Survivor[3]

Destiny's Child's lyrics around survival have been helpful to me personally over the years through heartbreak and adversity. Though as Meghan Markle famously pointed out, it's not enough to simply survive in life,[4] and it certainly isn't enough to just survive in the profession … Yes time and resources are in short supply, but our students deserve to interact with enthusiastic passionate professionals – not cynical individuals who are counting down to half-term (out loud!)

The difference between surviving and thriving in teaching has to come down to healthy habits – small daily acts that add up to overall well-being. Much in the same way that this book cannot address teacher well-being on the scale we'd like, nonetheless a piecemeal approach is a great place to start. So what healthy habits can we cultivate in order to thrive rather than survive?

It sounds obvious but sleep, diet and exercise are key: big aims which are a result of small incremental acts. I am well aware, however, that this is easier said than done especially in a job where our energy reserves are often supplemented by sugar and caffeine – and though this may work in the short term, this is unlikely to create the Beyoncé-esque longevity we're aiming for.

One incredibly admirable quality about Beyoncé is her discipline, and in order to keep ourselves well enough to thrive (rather than survive) we need self-discipline and self-care. If self-care sounds too indulgent, consider it as essential maintenance which will boost your efficacy and longevity. Self-care is not a bath and a face mask (but also, yes to this!), it is treating yourself with the reverence that you would care for someone you really love. So if (like me) you're at the bottom of a long list of people to feed/clothe/hydrate and generally *keep alive* you need to pull a Beyoncé and prioritise you.

In doing so, pay attention to what and who makes you feel good. Not alright or better but really, really good. When you have identified them, try to break them into small incremental habits so that you can access more of these in your daily life and practice. Research says that we can form a habit in as little as six weeks – around half a term. Further research shows that so-called habit stacking is more successful than trying to build a habit from scratch.[5] Habit stacking is where you add on the desired habit to something you routinely do at a set time. So for example if you always have a coffee in the morning and your desired habit is to be more hydrated, simply 'stack' a glass of water on to the habit you already have. Thus the habit you stack is more likely to stick.

Other stackable habits

- Getting fresh air
- Boosting your step count
- Consumption of fruit and veg
- Access to vitamin D
- A healthy sleep routine

Ultimately, your overall well-being cannot be solely futureproofed by small incremental habits – but it's a good place to start.

Win 2: Get in Formation[6]

Whether musically (Lady Gaga, Shakira, Jay-Z) or in an ambassadorial sense (L'Oréal, Pepsi, H&M), Beyoncé understands the importance of collaboration and working with others. There is no doubt that this is a massive contributory factor to maintaining your own well-being. Though interacting with colleagues can easily slide down the list of priorities, I would urge you to set time aside for this. Clearly, spending your planning and preparation time (PPA) discussing *Love Island* is not going to be better for your well-being than completing work you would otherwise have to complete at home – but do not underestimate the importance of collaborating with others, nor the impact this can have on your productivity.

Collaboration in schools works on a number of levels: firstly the opportunity to look out for your colleagues (and hopefully receive the same in return) is an incredibly useful tool. Similarly, when schools appoint a well-being lead who can feed back the overall feeling in the school – if there are common areas of consensus or workload triggers – this can be shared directly to the head to enable appropriate actions or amendments to take place.

Distributing workload is also another win for collaboration – both in the sense that two people sharing a high-pressure remit will feel half as burdened, but also because we can share planning/resources/curriculum plans. In the same way that Beyoncé sharing the lead vocals on 'Bills Bills Bills' with Kelly Rowland and Michelle Williams will have meant less time in the studio for each, collaboration is a powerful tool which can yield success on a far bigger scale.

Create a collaborative culture by:

▶ sharing resources freely with others

▶ adapting the work of others rather than starting from scratch

▶ challenging the need to reinvent the wheel

▶ prioritising joint planning where big tasks can be broken down into smaller component tasks.

Other reasons to collaborate (besides workload)

▶ It can foster higher levels of creativity and innovation.

▶ It can serve as excellent CPD for all parties.

▶ It can enable work to take place on a bigger scale and therefore amplify the impact of the work undertaken.

▶ It can impact positively on morale.

▶ It's an opportunity to network.

Collaboration needn't be limited within specific schools or trusts; it can be virtual, remote or national. In addition to the likes of Edutwitter, seeking out your opposite number in a different context is also a worthwhile endeavour which is likely to create longer term capacity (and possibly inspire and energise you in the short term). In the post-pandemic world it's easier than ever to collaborate because you don't even need to leave school in order for that to happen (though it'll likely have more impact if you can collaborate in person).

Ultimately, facilitating effective collaboration is a bit like a Beyoncé key change – it can take a bit of work to get there but it's absolutely glorious when you do.

Win 3: I'm (Sometimes) Sasha Fierce[7]

One of the notable things about Beyoncé is how much access and knowledge she gives the public. A strategy which likely started out as a marketing tool in order to create enigma offers us a good model for creating a healthy distance between professional personas and the real person beneath. Beyoncé created a stage alter ego Sasha Fierce and owns the fact that who we see on stage isn't really her authentic self.

Obviously, we should all strive to be authentic practitioners, not least of all because children and teenagers are the ultimate litmus test of sincerity. With this said, creating healthy distance between your true (and vulnerable) self and teacher you is a sound well-being strategy to safeguard your sense of self. By which I mean that although teaching is undoubtedly a 'work of heart', you need to have some emotional reserves because you never know when these are needed. For example, you might want your students to know that you love pets, but do they need to know the name of your beloved childhood pet – the mention of whom would guarantee an emotional response? While we need to connect and get to know our students, we must also be careful to avoid giving them emotional ammunition which could be used flippantly.

It's my experience that teachers are naturally approachable, but there is a difference between being approachable and being available: for example, being selective over who has your personal phone number or which WhatsApp groups you're in to enable you to engage with colleagues outside of working hours. It's also worth considering whether you engage in work phone calls and communication in the evenings. Of course, in extenuating circumstances this may be absolutely necessary and will depend upon your specific role – but habitual non-essential communication out of work hours should be avoided as much as possible.

Cultivating a professional alter ego is also an opportunity to emphasise the aspects of your practice you wish to role model to your students – your love of your subject and passion to make a difference should feature – but it's also an opportunity to model the healthy habits you'd like to instil in them. So do emphasise your resilience, ability to withstand pressure and dedication to your own well-being because these are qualities which students need to be taught and practise.

Your ideal professional alter ego should be:

- self-aware to know how they're perceived but secure enough not to give this too much credence
- outwardly positive at all times
- impervious to negative student feedback
- uber and unashamedly in love with learning (including your subject specialism where appropriate).

Other ways to be more Bey

- Use school breaks to unplug and recharge.
- Schedule time when you're not working (then own it and enjoy unapologetically!)
- Value yourself enough to ask to amend deadlines if this is needed.

▶ Invest in yourself – whether that's by completing CPD to upskill you, or by safeguarding time for something which will nourish you (which is not work!)

Memes tell us 'you have the same hours in a day as Beyoncé' – presumably intended to motivate us, rather than making us feel woefully inadequate. There is something truly inspirational about Beyoncé but it's not what she does in a day, it's what she's done for so long in her career – and the standard to which she's done it – which we should actually admire.

Beyoncé's career has spanned decades which have also seen seismic changes in attitudes towards race and gender, throughout which she has emerged as an extraordinary and unique artist, as a mother and icon; it's easy to see why she is widely considered to be one of the most influential artists of her generation.

Case Study

Mr R is a headteacher in a large inner-city Catholic Academy who has put well-being at the heart of his leadership and school, ultimately cultivating a culture in which healthy habits are prioritised and rewarded, enabling the longevity and resilience characterised by Beyoncé in this chapter. Upon joining the school as head, Mr R was surprised to find that his senior leadership team (SLT) would stay at school extremely late every night of the week – even Fridays. It seemed that they felt obliged to be seen to stay late and staying late had become a badge of honour. And a result the team weren't always working as productively as they could.

Mr R recognised that this practice had become an unhealthy habit which was detrimental to morale in the team and therefore to the overall well-being of the SLT. In addition to making it clear to all staff that they did not need to stay late at school needlessly, he also set out to model the healthy habits he wanted the staff to emulate, especially the SLT. More specifically, this included booking in personal training at 5pm every Friday – necessitating that he would have to be off-site by 4pm at the latest. This ensured that it wasn't just a preference but a pre-booked commitment for which he couldn't arrive late. Mr R then communicated this to SLT as a deliberate well-being strategy. This led to the team reflecting on their own un/healthy habits and question some long-held assumptions about leadership efficacy.

In being mindful and deliberate about his own time, and therefore the time of his SLT, Mr R slowly began to change the culture of the school and attitudes of the staff towards workload and time management. This was reinforced when he was given access to a leadership coach – dedicated, confidential and protected time to unpack and discuss emerging issues with an impartial expert felt revolutionary and enlightening. Such was the impact of leadership coaching on Mr R's own well-being, he facilitated the same

WELL-BEING WIN 1: BEYONCÉ AND HEALTHY HABITS

coaching for all senior leaders in his team, enabling them to have regular and meaningful access to the same service, which has since cascaded down to include key middle leaders. This was a high-level investment which required both funding and dedicated time in order to have impact.

The resulting impact of this is evident in the school's ethos which allows staff a reasonable amount of autonomy over when they work, ensuring that tasks which impact on students take priority over 'time thievery' exercises – and treating everyone's time as precious (including his own). In addition, a staff forum has been established in order to create an open dialogue between staff and leaders. This ensures that feedback around workload and well-being are reported directly to him. Additionally, there is a regular 'star of the week' item in staff briefing and half-termly prize draws for staff attendance to ensure that staff feel acknowledged and valued.

By showing that he could *listen* to staff and reminding them that they're only *irreplaceable* to their families and ultimately limiting the opportunities for *resentment*, Mr R was able to facilitate Beyoncé-esque levels of efficacy – which is surely to be applauded.

Look out for the Beyoncé archetype in your school/trust network and watch how they:

- ▶ work relentlessly in pursuit of excellence – while still maintain a sense of work/life balance
- ▶ unapologetically strive to achieve greatness without sacrificing their entire well-being
- ▶ are incredibly disciplined and committed practitioners
- ▶ do not hype their work (though others may!)
- ▶ are very unlikely to offer excuses instead of results.

Conversation Starters

Open the dialogue about healthy habits in your school by instigating the following conversations with your colleagues

What do you do just because it's good for you?

How do you prioritise exercise/hydration/meditation and still make such an impact?

I really admire your presence and contribution to the school, how do you preserve your energy?

Final Takeaway

Bey knows that power and performance are linked. In order to perform at Beyoncé-esque levels of efficacy, nourish and care for yourself like the superstar you surely are.

Notes

1. Jones, D. (2015) How Destiny's Child Changed R&B Forever. *Dazed Magazine*, 12 June. Available at www.dazeddigital.com/music/article/25044/1/how-destiny-s-child-changed-rb-forever (accessed 4 February 2023).
2. Hunt, E. (2016) Beyoncé's Lemonade Album Explained from Beginner to Beyhive. *The Guardian*, 29 April. Available at www.theguardian.com/music/2016/apr/29/beyonce-lemonade-jay-z-explainer (accessed 4 February 2023).
3. Destiny's Child (2001) Survivor. Texas: Columbia.
4. Quinn, D. (2019) Meghan Markle Opens up on 'Surviving as a New Royal'. *People Magazine*, 20 October. Available at people.com/royals/meghan-markle-never-thought-royal-life-would-be-easy/ (accessed 5 February 2023).
5. Scott, S.J. (2014) *Habit Stacking: 97 Small Life Changes That Take Five Minutes or Less.* Create Space Independent Publishers.
6. Beyoncé (2026) Formation. New York: Columbia.
7. Beyoncé (2008) I am … Sasha Fierce. Los Angeles: Columbia.

WELL-BEING WIN 2

A Chapter by Charlotte

Robbie Williams and Resourcefulness

[verb] The process of using contacts and drawing on expertise and ideas to achieve outcomes.

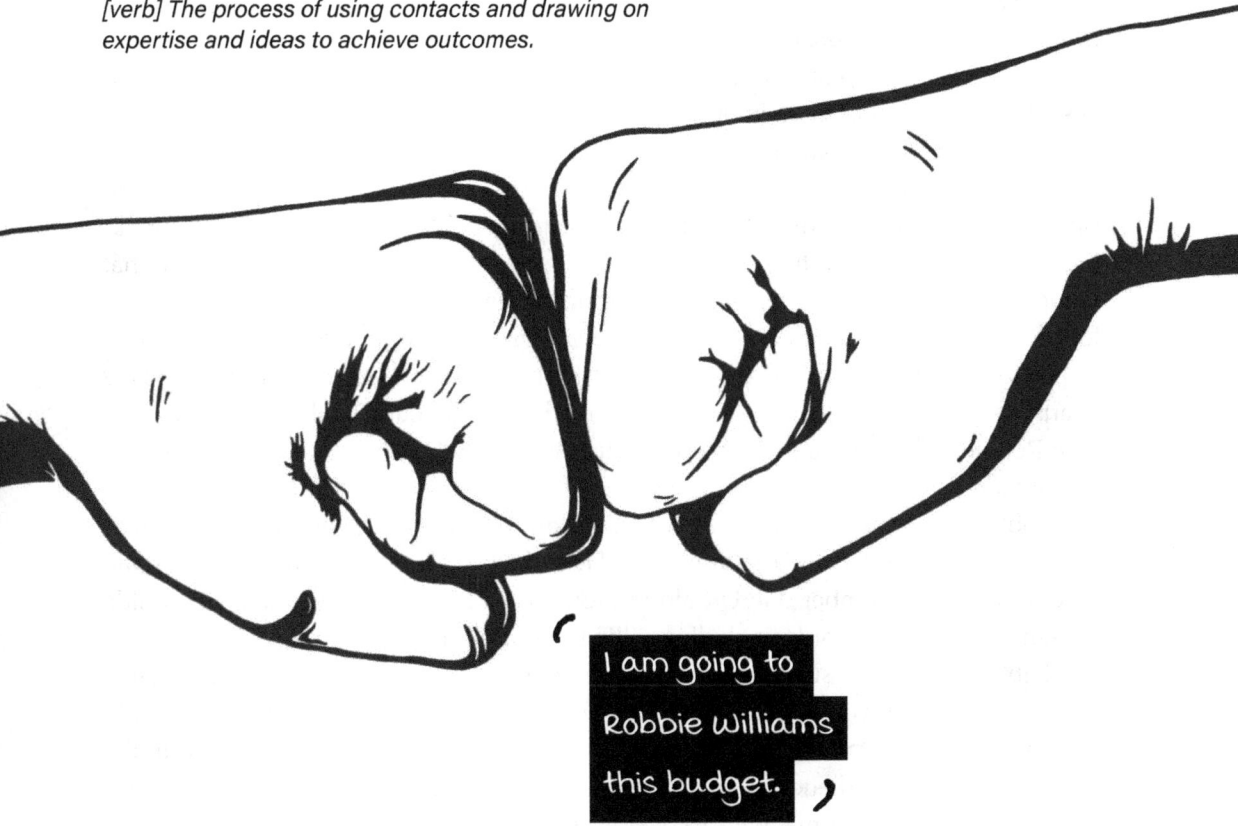

Background

As a genuine fan and as someone who is proud to be from the city of Stoke-on-Trent, it is a great pleasure and delight to write about one of my favourite icons, Robbie Williams.

One of the many things that I love about the city where my roots are so firmly ingrained is that a lot of people claim to have 'Robbie links and connections'! Many of us are genuinely proud of his achievements and lots of Stokies have met him (or maybe seen him at least). The first time I saw him play live was probably unapologetically one of the best days of my life and his homecoming gig even more so! (After my wedding day of course – I will make sure that's in the book!) He truly adds to a tapestry of creativity in a city that needs putting on the map. Robbie has helped to do this and I am so thankful.

Robbie Williams was born in Stoke-on-Trent on 13 February 1974 and followed in his father's footsteps, developing a true love of music and performing from a very young age.[1] It was evident that through being surrounded by music, stand-up and performances he was inspired to venture onto the stage. In an MTV documentary, Robbie's mother tells of a three-and-a-half-year-old Robert performing when on holiday to hundreds of families. She said from that moment it was clear that he belonged in the limelight and most of all, he enjoyed every minute.[2]

He spent many days at the Red Lion pub in Burslem town centre, watching his dad sing, and in his own words Robbie said, 'I remember looking at the people, then looking [at my dad on stage], then looking at the people again and wanting them to do that to me'.[3] He craved that audience and engagement with a crowd. That dream came true for him and between 1990 and 1995 at the young age of only sixteen he found fame as part of the boy band Take That – one of the most famous bands of all time. Many hearts were broken (including my own!) when he left the band in the mid-1990s, but then Robbie redefined himself as a solo artist, selling millions of copies of albums and sell-out tours.[4]

Robbie has won more BRIT Awards than any other artist in history and in 2023 received the prestigious BRIT Icon Award.[5] He is the best-selling British solo artist of all time. His thirteen number one UK albums (only Elvis Presley ties with this), alongside a plethora of world records, including selling the most tickets (1.6 million) in one day, highlight his enormous success as both a live performer and a recording artist.[6] Playing to millions at Knebworth, Glastonbury and various worldwide tours,[7] he has brought musical talent, entertainment and, at times, an almost theatrical performance from the stage to many. His audience are mesmerised by his musicality, but it's his mischievous personality and humour that wins us over every time too.

It has not always been an easy road for Robbie though. He has found himself in some difficulties due to battling excessive drinking, taking drugs and allowing fame to spiral out of control, often making the headlines in the process. He has ventured

WELL-BEING WIN 2: ROBBIE WILLIAMS AND RESOURCEFULNESS

down dark paths, having to check into rehabilitation because of addiction to prescription drugs and alcohol, his mental health at rock bottom as a result. Thankfully, he has come out of the dark tunnel and through the other side, marrying Ayda Field in 2010 and is now enjoying being a dad to four children.[8]

Within his social media platforms, interviews and tours, Robbie admits to also being addicted to success, rather than simply the celebrity status. He still remains humble, despite his assured, charismatic and confident exterior, often stating that he feels apprehensive before performing, but the moment he steps out onto the stage, he knows that being in the spotlight is where he belongs.

As well as his renowned performances, tours, singing and songwriting, Robbie's philanthropy is inspiring. He is a passionate footballer and Port Vale supporter. His homecoming gig at the Vale Park in 2022 raised money for two local charities, the Donna Louise Trust and the Hubb Foundation, and his fantastic work with Soccer Aid has raised over £30 million for UNICEF over a number of years.[9]

He is still performing, but values family time the most.

Win 1: Let Me Entertain You![10]

Enjoy the job you do

A natural born entertainer, Robbie Williams knows how to win over a crowd. Some say that he oozes arrogance, some say that it's charisma and, for many, he is undeniably a confident and a captivating performer from humble beginnings who loves what he does and works hard at it. This creativity and passion make him adore his job more and more over time. He truly is obsessed with performing.

Teaching is hard work, but it's also the best job in the world. We have the opportunity to educate and impart knowledge to our young people. Why wouldn't we have fun with it? Learning to laugh at yourself and entertain – whether through humour, creative thinking or artistic means – is vital. It is this resourcefulness that inspires, motivates and captures learners' imaginations. I still recall a lot of my time at school because I am lucky and thoroughly enjoyed it, but the lessons and moments that really stand out to me are those unique and creative ones. This made revision a lot easier and a whole lot more manageable!

Other ways in which we can successfully work together ... and entertain!

▶ Don't take yourself too seriously! Things go wrong and that's fine. If we have the ability to laugh at ourselves and entertain, it shows self-assurance and confidence, but also a sense of happiness and well-rounded feeling of well-being.

WELL-BEING WIN 2: ROBBIE WILLIAMS AND RESOURCEFULNESS

▶ Have fun – teaching is the best job. We get to work with children and young people who have the ability to change the world. Have fun with them, make them smile, make them laugh.

▶ Work well and effectively with others, but also know that you can do it on your own. We may never know the full story about the Take That fall-out and then the reuniting … and then the return to solo performance again, but we can categorically state that Robbie was a huge success in a band and a huge success as a solo artist.

▶ Know your strengths, play to those, but also know the strengths of others and utilise these. This effective collaboration will have positive results and also make you realise that there is no need to do it all. Staff and colleagues are your most valuable resource.

▶ Enjoy and embrace the challenges: even the GCSE pressures, the SATS (standard attainment tests) stresses, the marking. Remember the reason why you went into this profession and avoid getting too pressured by the things that do not matter in the long run.

Win 2: Let Love Be Your Energy[11]

Always work with compassion and use this as the foundation for your work and creation. This is essentially the most impactful approach for an individual's well-being. Robbie's song 'Let Love be Your Energy' should speak to all of us!

I attended a coaching CPD session on the power of words back in 2021 and the whole concept resonated with me considerably. The way in which we speak and communicate to others is pivotal and individuals never forget how you made them feel. The best and most impactful leaders and teachers are those who are compassionate and always show care and love in everything they do. Striving for this to permeate within our practice is a good ambition to have.

Sometimes, we have to appear to be stricter, providing firm boundaries for young people who may need it, and we may even have to have courageous conversations with pupils, families or colleagues. The way in which these are conducted makes a huge difference to both your own and others' well-being. Remember this.

Tools to help us to act with compassion

▶ We don't always know what people are going through. We may have to have a conversation with a pupil who is misbehaving, or perhaps as a middle or senior leader we have noticed that a colleague is underperforming and standards are slipping. We should make no apology for having high expectations or high standards, but often there is a reason for people and pupils' struggling. Be kind. Pose the question 'what do you need?'; ask if people are ok and truly mean it, as well as thank people for their contribution. It's surprising what conversations can flow when compassion and trust are firm foundations. (See also the Marcus Rashford chapter for more on the power of compassion.)

- Have faith in people and state this. If members of a team, including children, feel micromanaged, this can have a negative impact on well-being. Allow people to give their ideas, pose suggestions and feel heard.
- Share your objectives and vision, form positive relationships and take people with you rather than working against them.
- Recognise that we work with human beings and complex emotions. Sometimes we all need a pick-me-up!

Win 3: Kids[12]

As mentioned above, Robbie's generosity to charities over the years spanning over his career has been apparent, many of which focus on supporting children and families. As teachers, every decision, every moment, every resource, every spend should be focused on the child. It is very easy within teaching to become overwhelmed by the little things – looming deadlines, a busy school calendar – but we should always focus on the pupils in our care, something that most chapters will keep coming back to and rightly so!

We entered this profession to educate young people. We should want to give all children the best opportunities in life and inspire them to achieve – both personally and academically. More than ever, however, our role is so beyond teaching: it is focused on social care, nurture and support in its different forms. It can be difficult to not get stressed or overwhelmed at times.

How many times though have we been guilty of spending too long on tasks or decisions that actually may not directly benefit the pupils? How many times have we lost sight of what truly counts? How many meetings have been spent discussing things that are in fact not pupil-centred or not even relevant at all?

We should be open to anything if it benefits our young people. Late nights spent planning a lesson that you just *know* Year 6 are going to love, months spent planning that epic residential for Year 9 – the first time the students had left the town they live in – or the weekend/holiday revision sessions for your GCSE group: no, we don't mind doing any of these for the kids!

Other ways we can ensure that there is a pupil-centred approach in school

▶ The power of pupil voice is integral. Ensure that you have pupil leaders and/or a school council to make sure that they speak out and make suggestions on change.

▶ Every task that you undertake should begin with the question: 'what's in it for the children?' It will honestly help to re-evaluate, prioritise and, most likely, save time.

▶ Encourage extra-curricular and enrichment opportunities and be a part of this. The reward you get seeing the children grow academically is powerful, but seeing them grow into young people and foster a new talent or develop confidence is invaluable too.

▶ Do not be afraid to challenge if something is detrimental to pupils. Do not 'settle' or quietly go along with something if you know that the pupils are not gaining.

▶ Be the best teacher, leader, mentor you can be for *them*! But that also means looking after yourself too. You will be able to give more if you do.

An individual level

▶ Even if you don't feel confident, sometimes *acting* confident and performing will help. Use this creativity to change your mindset. Someone once said to me that 'teaching is a little bit like acting'. When we don't feel 100% due to the half-term colds and lurgy, we still need to act like we are to win over our pupils. They rely on us. Having this 'performer's mindset' will strangely help with our well-being. Try it!

▶ Give a bit back to others. When you have achieved a dream, succeeded in a particular area or tackled a problem and challenge, help others and give something back to support your peers.

▶ Work effectively with others as a team, celebrate and acknowledge individual talents and play to strengths, but make no apology for having your own targets, goals and dreams and be open about this.

▶ It takes a lot, but ask for help when needed. Reach out and embrace the work and influence of others that may be able to enhance your practice further.

A whole-school level

▶ Is confidence celebrated in your school culture, or is it labelled as 'arrogance'? There is a difference! Encouraging confidence and self-belief among staff and pupils is so important … and not squashing this is even more valuable. Ignore the negative voices and critics and create a confident, self-assured culture within your school setting. After all, we should be teaching our children that they are capable of anything, so why should we stop here and not encourage one another?

- ▶ Is there a culture of effective feedback or comments that empowers others or destroys them? Leaders having an 'open door' policy where possible will assist with this and create transparency
- ▶ Is there a culture of individuals taking things too seriously, or is there a balance of fun, even in the stressful times? Ensure that there is joy permeating through every element of school life where possible. I would rather default to humour most of the time! No one will be disappointed with this intent

Look out for Robbie-like resourceful entertainers in your school or trust and observe how they:

- ▶ are extroverts in nature, but reflect and always look to better themselves
- ▶ like a challenge – even when it makes them feel nervous or pushed out of their comfort zone, they accept it and perform (think Robbie Williams at Knebworth!)
- ▶ give to others in need and take pleasure and have great gains in supporting others
- ▶ know their roots, know where they have come from … as well as where they are going
- ▶ do not apologise or downplay achievements.

Case Study

Mrs B is currently in her twentieth year as a teacher with ten years at her first school and ten years at her current.

A talented and driven primary school teacher, as well as an ambitious and aspiring leader, she became SENCO in the May of her first year, progressing toward Phase Leader at the end of her fourth year. Next, she became Deputy Headteacher and then moved on a secondment to her current larger school. During this time, she moved to Head of School and gained her first substantive headship just over three years ago.

She has the mantra that every day working in education (particularly in a headship role) is rewarding and challenging, which makes each of us stronger as a leader and this overall, helps us with our well-being. She particularly recalls how the challenges of leading and teaching throughout the pandemic were difficult for all schools. We all had to be resourceful in the way that lessons were taught, obtaining laptops and other resources for the children, which at times were a logistical nightmare. However, coming together as a strong team, ensuring that the pupils were at the core of everything helped her and her school community to prioritise and maintain the balance of education and nurture, assisting with every stakeholder's well-being.

WELL-BEING WIN 2: ROBBIE WILLIAMS AND RESOURCEFULNESS

In relation to resourcefulness, her first year as a substantive headteacher was certainly a time when this was more crucial than ever. Mrs B talks about how she works with the school business manager to set the budget for each academic year. A recent example of saving money, but also utilising your most valuable resource, the staff, comes to mind:

> Moving an existing staff member into a different key stage where a vacancy had become available was a way of not only using existing resources, but playing to strengths, which overall led to better outcomes for learners.

She stated that 'through working as a trust, we can gain positive discounts when purchasing resources, SLAs and sustain together. This has positively impacted on our school budgets ensuring pupils are always at the very heart of every school decision.' Overall, well-being is prioritised for all – the staff are working to strengths, there was no need for restructures or redundancies and within the financial climate that they were experiencing, this was definitely something they wished to avoid. Also, the Head and Finance Team are able to sleep soundly knowing that the school is not in a financial crisis.

Knowing that decisions are never simply down to just one person – even as the headteacher – is reassuring and calms well-being. The mental health of pupils and staff is crucial to all schools and it is important that staff and pupils feel listened to. If the leaders in school prioritise well-being and model this, then the rest is more likely to fall into place. The school also has a well-being group, which ensures that staff contribute to items such as workload and organise social events to bring staff together. This overall togetherness is key in creating a sense of togetherness and by having a school 'family' approach it has led to longevity of staff, productivity and resourcefulness, which is invaluable.

Talking Points

Open the dialogue about well-being and resourcefulness through the following methods

- Speaking to the pupils! This sounds so obvious, but what do they feel they need in school at the moment? We may not be able to promise a lifetime of no homework and billions of pounds spent on FA-standard, Wembley-Stadium-sized football pitches, but they often have the best ideas and make the best suggestions. Have a school council and opportunity for pupil voice forum and give them the stage.
- As mentioned above, a question that should often be asked as a leader is 'what do you need?': allowing people to truly reflect on what is necessary to help them and their practice is priceless. It also helps individuals to prioritise.

Talk about 'time investment' and avoid time thievery. If a new initiative is not an investment for our young people, then rethink. If a new idea is simply going to be onerous and detrimental for staff well-being and for little or no gain, it's a 'no'.

Be creative and look at other ways of doing things. Take risks if it means greater resourcefulness in the long run.

Overall, always ask: 'how will the children benefit?'

Final Takeaway

Resourcefulness is not just about money; it's about time investment too and ensuring that time is saved, protected and utilised wisely. Ultimately, every decision that is made in school must have the young people in our care at the centre. Using resources such as the Department for Education's Schools' Financial Benchmarking website[13] as a tool for comparative budgetary information, as well as the Education Endowment Foundation's toolkit[14] to inform decisions, particularly about cost and impact, are invaluable methods and aid strategic thinking, not just for leaders, but all practitioners.

Knowing that the impact of tough decisions is for the gain of pupils will mean that our mental health as teachers and leaders is more effectively balanced. Always remember this, be confident in your thinking, own that stage… and you won't go wrong!

Notes

1 Williams, R. (2020) Robbie Williams Biography. Available at www.biography.com/musician/robbie-williams (accessed 4 November 2023).
2 Williams, R. (2019) Robbie Williams Essential MTV Special. Available at https://www.youtube.com/watch?v=nK58_RHVZ-4 (accessed 4 November 2023).
3 Ibid.
4 Ibid.
5 BRIT Awards. (2023) Robbie Williams. Available at www.brits.co.uk/news/robbie-williams-honoured-with-the-brits-icon-award (accessed 7 November 2023).
6 Williams, R. (2023) Robbie Williams Official Website Timeline. Available at https://robbiewilliams.com/pages/timeline (accessed 4 November 2023).
7 Ibid.
8 Ibid.
9 Williams, R. (2023) Robbie Williams Official Website News. Available at: https://robbiewilliams.com/blogs/news (accessed 4 November 2023).

10　Williams, R. and Chambers, G. (1997) Let Me Entertain You. London: Chrysalis.
11　Williams, R., Chambers, G. and Power, S. (2001) Let Love Be Your Energy. London: Chrysalis.
12　Williams, R. and Minogue, K. (2000) Kids. London: Chrysalis.
13　Department for Education (2023) Schools Financial Benchmarking. Available at https://schools-financial-benchmarking.service.gov.uk/ (accessed 4 November 2023).
14　Education Endowment Foundation. (2023) Teaching and Learning Toolkit. Available at https://educationendowmentfoundation.org.uk/education-evidence/teaching-learning-toolkit (accessed 4 November 2023).

WELL-BEING WIN 3

A Chapter by Charlotte

Dame Kelly Holmes and Resilience

[adjective] An inner strength and resilience that leads to the achievement of goals and ambitions.

> *It was a Dame Kelly Holmes interview. mission accomplished!*

WELL-BEING WIN 3: DAME KELLY HOLMES AND RESILIENCE

Background

Dame Kelly Holmes is well known for her talent in running – to say the least! – and specifically for winning Olympic Gold in both the 800m and 1500m at the 2004 Athens Games, securing her place in history as the first female British athlete to do so, inspiring many to follow her career path in the process. She participated in the Olympics, Worlds, Commonwealth Games and Europeans,[1] living out her passion and love for running and displaying a dedication and commitment that, in itself, was record breaking!

At the age of seventeen, despite her ability in running going from strength to strength, she paused this career to enter the military, but returned to the track in 1992.[2] A few years on, she established the Dame Kelly Holmes Trust, with a vision to utilise the skills of athletes to grow and empower young people, many of whom may have been faced with adversity and challenges in their path. The Trust's mission is simply that everyone deserves to have a 'champion in [their] corner'.[3]

Through effective mentoring programmes the Trust encourages young people to strive to become the best version of themselves, rebuilding lives and providing individuals with opportunities and chances. Through providing inspirational role models, encouraging a positive outlook and building resilience, this is achieved and the impact can be phenomenal. Utilising the skills of athletes and recognising how these traits are transferrable helps in achieving such goals and, just potentially, has the ability to create stars for the future through effectively fostering those talents.[4]

The reason that Kelly has a desire to help, support, mentor and inspire others in the industry is because of her own battles that she has faced over the years. She can empathise and relate in many ways and perhaps even more inspiring than her Olympic golds is Kelly speaking out after a thirty-four-year-old silence about her sexuality. An article for *The Guardian* in June 2022 highlighted that she said:

> I needed to do this now, for me … It was my decision. I'm nervous about saying it. I feel like I'm going to explode with excitement. Sometimes I cry with relief. The moment this comes out, I'm essentially getting rid of that fear.[5]

After being consumed by fear as a young adult, due to the fact that being gay was illegal in the army, only close family and friends knew this. She admitted to feeling isolated and even having suicidal thoughts because no one in sport at the time spoke about this. Her strength in speaking out after years of being crippled by fear made her at last feel 'finally free'. In an television interview, captured in *The Daily Mail* in July 2023, she describes the intensity of that fear:

> I was raided. The Royal Military Police would come into my bedroom and ransack it completely, I was scared. I was 23. I was petrified. I didn't want to lose my career,' she continued.[6]

WELL-BEING WIN 3: DAME KELLY HOLMES AND RESILIENCE

> I had to hide letters from my sister and my friends in the boot of my car in case they accused me of being gay.[7]
>
> It caused me mental health issues throughout my whole career because I was so petrified. The shame of being gay was institutionally driven into me. I realised I was gay when I joined, that's why I didn't come out until last year.[8]

A true powerhouse of a woman whose inner strength, physical and mental resilience are incomprehensible, Dame Kelly Holmes is a true heroine. Like many of the icons we reference, she was from very humble beginnings, grew up on a council estate and also spent time in care. As a young girl, she had low confidence and self-esteem, believing that she was not good enough and would not achieve. It was a supportive PE teacher who recognised her ability and talent and Kelly often references this as a pivotal point for her in life. The power of someone believing in you, building your confidence and making you believe in *yourself* is invaluable. As teachers and educationists, this is a heart-warming tale.

She is a true icon and inspiration in the sporting world, but ultimately, she sets a positive example to everyone and encourages people to simply be themselves. Her mantra of dedication, resilience and celebrating your uniqueness are strategies that many of us can take away with us. I hope that we will!

Win 1: 'Believing in yourself is vital if you want to achieve the very best out of life'

Kelly's autobiography, *Black, White and Gold*, very openly addresses her difficult childhood and struggles with mental health and her low self-esteem, but also the power that positivity can have on us.[9] Her PE teacher was the first person to encourage her and recognise her amazing ability and gift. In time, this then encouraged her to believe that what she had was a true talent, which she later pursued and achieved greatness through her dedication and hard work.

Her book is raw; organically and honestly talking about her far from luxurious and privileged life. It is fantastic reading for anyone with an interest in sport, particularly running, but more than that, it highlights how anyone can pursue a dream and finally be confident and happy with who they are.

As teachers, leaders and people who work in education, we are so focused on improving the confidence of the young people in our care (or we certainly should be!). Making children believe that everyone should have a dream, set goals and with hard work and faith they can be achieved is surely a fantastic mantra for future generations and at the heart of many mission statements of schools. However, something happens to us as teenagers and into adulthood – imposter syndrome kicks in and sometimes into full force! We question decisions after once being carefree and, overall, lose faith in ourselves, many people simply 'coasting'. I think many will know what I am talking about.

We instil a sense of self-belief and confidence in young people through effective pastoral care, appropriate feedback in teaching and learning and, overall, positive relationships with pupils who we work with. We must model this with each other too! Leaders should empower staff and, actually vice versa. Imagine creating a culture where feedback is positive, appreciated, constructive and leads to individuals believing in themselves. Anything is possible …

Other ways and strategies that will help us to 'believe in ourselves'

▶ Keep a diary or a list of things that you have achieved. This may be something as simple as a pupil finally grasped that maths equation, or maybe they finally spoke to you about something that was on their mind. Perhaps you absolutely aced a lesson and loved delivering it. These are everyday wins – celebrate them!

▶ Empower others and be positive with colleagues – by praising others it creates a *culture* of positivity, which only grows and blooms.

▶ Recognise that we are only human and not every day will be smooth. Every day is a new one; in fact, every *moment* is a new one. Don't let a 'bad moment' or negative experience define *you*

Win 2: 'I think that people realise that I am happy with what I have achieved'

There is nothing wrong with having confidence. In fact, it is a gift. Unfortunately, some confuse this gift with arrogance, which is so starkly different. Being proud of achievements and goals is something very special and also helps to inspire others to do the same, overall normalising self-belief.

Kelly has opened up about how she was riddled with self-doubt but applied strategies to tackle this, recognising that actually she has worked very hard over the years, driven by commitment, a genuine love for what she does and resilience. This has led to her success, encouraging many to follow her footsteps, working hard for their dreams and ambitions.

Imagine if we took the time to feel proud of ourselves. Again, for those working in schools it is very easy to feel engulfed by guilt. We can focus so much on the children in our care or colleagues whom we line manage that we do not take time for us. As a result, we are then not reflecting on just how far we have come. Every week, no matter what your role in a school, you have the potential to win hearts and minds. You have the potential to impart wisdom and to see young people grow and flourish. This is SUCH an achievement! In the fast-paced nature of our work we can often choose to ignore this or fail to recognise the value. Be happy with what you achieve – even those 'little wins'.

Kelly has achieved so much: an Olympic gold medallist, founder of the Dame Kelly Holmes Trust, inspiring young people from disadvantaged backgrounds, shaping their lives and driving ambition. She has spoken openly and honestly about her sexuality and the adversity surrounding this as a teenager and, in her book, also written describing feelings of loss and grief. She has not let these challenges define her – quite the opposite. She is proud of how far she has come and how she never gave up. Focus on the wins, but also to focus on how the journey getting there is also crucial.

Other ways to be proud of what we achieve

It can be difficult 'bigging ourselves up' at times, often labelling what we do as 'just a job', but often self-care can come in the form of just recognition for oneself and celebrating how far we have come.

- ▶ Define what 'success' means to you, Learning and accomplishment appear in many different forms. Sometimes it may be very much a drive towards headship or a new job role and challenge … and another day it may look like completing the marking of a pile of English GCSE mock papers that have been furiously building up. Either way, both are worthy of recognition.
- ▶ Set daily or weekly goals and tick them off when accomplished. The sense of completion and accomplishment can really give you a boost, lead to better physical and mental health and help to build resilience.
- ▶ Having faith in our ability and being proud is not conceited or egotistical; it shows that we have some balance and compassion for ourselves. In a world where 'well-being' seems to appear on every agenda, we still don't all seem to have this grasped; however, it is vital!

Win 3: 'When you cross the finish line, it is a wonderful feeling. It's hard to describe'[10]

Many trainees or teachers new to the profession endure late nights ensuring that files of evidence are pristine and perhaps initially take hours to just plan one lesson. Observations as an early career teacher and acting on feedback, the parents' evenings, first time organising school trips, presenting to governors and staff and juggling teaching and learning with the pastoral care and sleepless nights worrying about some pupils that you just can't shake out of your head – teaching and educational leadership have many layers, but my goodness, they are so rewarding! The sense of pride when you teach your first official lesson as a qualified teacher and having your own classes are definitely worth the hard work.

We have to pause and remember this when the stresses of Ofsted are rife or when we're clinging on to the holidays, not yet psychologically prepared for our summer haze to be over. However, we love what we do and working with children and young people really is the best job in the world.

This viewpoint is very much a Kelly-ism. She would honestly admit that it has not been plain-sailing for her, with injuries, mental health battles, loss and criticism. Her success has not come easy, being born into a disadvantaged background, finding her way and overcoming struggles. She admits that '[she] used to wash cars, clean windows, go shopping for the old people across the road who would throw 50p out of the window. And … was quite happy with that. Because [she] was helping people and it taught [her] about the value of money and trying to find … own opportunities.'[11]

Remembering the why is powerful. It reminds us of our roots, the reasons why we do what we do and, overall, gives us a sense of pride. It is often the most challenging things that reap the most reward.

An individual level

- Never lose that sense of ambition and aspiration, but be clear on what this means for you. Keep a journal to mark the journey on how you got there – it may just be a best seller one day!
- Do not let a negative moment, day or experience define you. Storms pass and if you allow them, the more challenging experiences will channel an energy or accomplishment in a positive way. Go for it!
- Be glad of what you have achieved, how far you have come and do not feel guilty for celebrating such wins. Self-care is important and helps to restore balance and well-being, which, overall, makes us more productive in the workplace
- Accept praise and compliments. It is often deemed as rude or impolite to accept such comments. In fact, they are gifts and what do we say when given a gift? 'Thank you!'

A whole-school level

- How is feedback given and shared at your place of work? Is it through processes that empower people, encourage, offer mentoring and support… or does it actually knock confidence, leading to a culture of low morale and mood? Make the change.
- Is progress rewarded and for all stakeholders? Is everyone acknowledged and is it recognised that success, learning and positive results look different for different people? Something to think about …

- Is there a culture and ethos of aspiration, or it coasting and complacency?
- Is individuality and creativity encouraged and are leaders open to new ideas and initiatives?

Look how Dame Kelly Holmes supporters do the following

- Do not accept things for free! They work incredibly hard and achieve based on their own merit rather than being reliant on luck.
- They display a healthy competition with themselves, wanting to better their practice and develop, rather than coast or sail through.
- They champion others and encourage success, genuinely being happy for other people and their achievements. They take great pleasure in seeing others succeed.
- They want to help people, using their own experiences to support and speak out.
- They embrace challenges and are more 'glass half full' than 'glass half empty'. They look back at adversity and difficulties as opportunities and character shaping moments.

Case Study

Miss D has been teaching for fifteen years in secondary education, and has been a middle leader in a pastoral role for six years of that time. She is an icon in her own right and one of the most resilient leaders I have ever had the pleasure to work with.

She describes how middle leadership and her role has changed so much over a period of a few years:

> During my time as a middle leader in secondary education I have seen the role grow significantly and with that growth the pressures put on all of us middle leaders have dramatically increased. My most challenging times have arisen from the sheer amount of workload generated from my middle leader role.

She describes middle leadership as very much a 'think on your feet' role and how it's true that no two days are the same – this is of course what makes the job so interesting – but the balance of teaching full time and working as a middle leader in charge of pastoral provision for students has been testing. There will always be a handful of students who dominate your time, and her most challenging moments were connected to one student and their family in particular:

> The sheer volume of issues and subsequent contact with home increased my workload beyond what I had ever known – this one student and their needs

resulted in me wanting to step down from a role I love. Just as I had cleared the decks of the issues accumulated from one week, more headed my way that I needed to invest time in – I headed for the office of my school's principal and announced I was quitting the role. We spoke in a frank manner, and I was encouraged to carry on with some supportive measures in place. I prioritised what I needed to do and admitted I couldn't do it all. I also accepted the support from fellow middle leaders. I am glad I didn't give up.

Miss D highlights how vital communication is and how 'communicating in a clear and respectful manner to colleagues is the best approach when facing moments that test us.' It is easy to assume that those who can help you know what is going on. As teachers we often smile through the day and remain calm, but our colleagues won't know what the issue is if we don't share what is troubling us or what we are finding a challenge.

Everyone has difficult times and working in education is a highly stressful and challenging environment to be in. She advises accepting support from others and also that being a supportive colleague to those who work alongside you is invaluable. Teaching and educational leadership can sometimes be an isolated affair – the classroom door closes, and you are alone for most of the day (albeit with your students) – share your highs and your lows with those you work with.

Even the most serene, relaxed and rational leaders can be tested. Miss D's words of wisdom to others would be to remain calm, seek to prioritise your work, and pause and think before you make those bigger decisions. She admits that in this scenario, and others besides, 'sleeping on it' really can give clarity.

Schools are vast institutions and it's easy to assume that others know you are struggling and are wilfully allowing you to. Do not assume this. Talk with colleagues. Talk to your leadership group. Accept any support that is offered and, once back on track, be that supportive hand for others! Taking care of yourself and others, being honest and effectively communicating with others all make you a resilient leader and, overall, leads to a more well-rounded and balanced sense of well-being.

Talking Points

Raise the profile of resilience in school through the following measures

Spending quality time with colleagues and having opportunities to make suggestions and to feel 'heard'.

Be visionary and share that vision – whatever your role in school, do your pupils know this? Can they articulate this?

Recognise when someone is struggling and offer to mentor, support … make them a brew! Mostly, recognise when you yourself are struggling, sleep on decisions so that irrational outcomes are not met and ask for what you feel is needed and what you think will help and support you. There is absolutely no shame in this. In fact, it truly makes you stronger.

Final Takeaway

Day and Qu (2014) highlight that resilience is not an innate quality, but a 'product of personal and professional dispositions and values and socially constructed.' They elaborate by stating that 'it develops along with and manifests itself as a result of a dynamic process within a given context.'[12]

In order to *build* resilience we actually need to ensure that we communicate and share where possible. Often lightening the burden will prevent us from being held back and, consequentially, help us to become better practitioners. Being open and transparent is so important and welcoming support from others enables us as teachers and leaders to be more likely to model this to others and be that support to individuals with whom we work. One step at a time we will create a culture of resilient teachers and leaders and mostly, a culture of openness: well-being, of course, being prioritised in the process.

Notes

1. Dame Kelly Holmes Trust website (2023) Available at: www.damekellyholmestrust.org/dame-kelly-holmes (accessed 4 November 2023).
2. Ibid.
3. Ibid.
4. Ibid.
5. Booth, R. (2022) Kelly Holmes Comes Out As Gay: 'I Needed to Do This Now, For Me'. *The Guardian*, 19 June. Available at www.theguardian.com/sport/2022/jun/19/kelly-holmes-comes-out-gay-lesbian-army (accessed 4 November 2023).
6. Parkin, L. (2023) Dame Kelly Holmes Gets Emotional As She Discusses Horrific Army 'Witch Hunt' During LGBT Ban That Left Her With 'Mental Health Issues'. *The Daily Mail*, 21 July. Available at: www.dailymail.co.uk/tvshowbiz/article-12324425/Dame-Kelly-Holmes-gets-emotional-discusses-horrific-army-witch-hunt-LGBT-ban-left-mental-health-issues.html (accessed 4 November 2023).
7. Ibid.

8 Ibid.
9 Holmes, K. (2008) *Black, White and Gold*. Virgin Books.
10 Inspirational Stories. (2020) Kelly Holmes Quotes. Available at www.inspirationalstories.com/quotes/kelly-holmes-when-you-cross-the-line-it-is/ (accessed 4 November 2023).
11 Lobb, A. (2021) Dame Kelly Holmes: 'Believing in Yourself Is So Powerful'. Available at www.bigissue.com/news/dame-kelly-holmes-believing-in-yourself-is-so-powerful/ (accessed 5 February 2024).
12 Day, C. and Gu, Q. (2014) *Resilient Teachers, Resilient Schools: Building and Sustaining Quality in Testing Times*. Routledge (p. 11).

WELL-BEING WIN 4

A Chapter by Tracey

Stephen Hawking and Pressure

[adjective] the property of withstanding pressure without crumbling.

The run-up to SATs feels a bit Stephen Hawking

WELL-BEING WIN 4: STEPHEN HAWKING AND PRESSURE

Professor Stephen Hawking's destiny as a cosmologist seems to have been fated on the day he was born: exactly 300 years to the day since the death of the astronomer Galileo. After an esteemed and trailblazing career in academia, Stephen Hawking died in 2018 leaving behind a body of work which ultimately brought us closer to understanding the mysteries of the universe – serving as a fittingly inextinguishable legacy.[1]

Despite emanating from academic lineage – both his mother and father were Cambridge graduates – few could have predicted the impact that Stephen would have on the world, nor the obstacles he would overcome in order to achieve this. Born in Oxford during World War II, Stephen was the oldest of four siblings and while initially academically unremarkable, he was noted for his thirst for knowledge and innate curiosity – skills which later propelled him into (and enabled) his greatness within the field of academic research.[2]

Had he not become unwell, Stephen and his work would still have been remembered as seminal. However, Stephen's legacy isn't just as a theoretical physicist or academic, but in his doggedly tenacious response to the diagnosis of motor neurone disease, where he redefined disability.[3] Though it's well documented that at the time of his diagnosis aged just twenty-two his prognosis was bleak – doctors told him that he wasn't likely to live beyond a few years – it's fair to say that him revolutionising the field of astrophysics was somewhat unexpected. However, after publishing his groundbreaking research into black holes, Stephen lived to do just that.[4] In doing so he gave hope to those living with disabilities that they could do more than merely manage: they could actually change the world.

Stephen married his first wife Jane in 1965 shortly after his diagnosis, and they had three children together: Robert, Lucy and Timothy. They were married for thirty years, during which time it was clear that his initial prognosis was not quite as bleak as first assumed and that he was determined to function not only as a world-renowned physicist but also as a father. He was later married to Elaine Mason from 1995 to 2006.[5]

Ironically (or perhaps fittingly) as Stephen's condition grew worse – effectively leaving him paralysed and unable to speak – his profile within academia was catapulted onto a rapid upward trajectory. Stephen went on to utilise technology for over fifty years which enabled him to continue his work, his eventual inability to walk or speak only seemed to make him more determined to persist in his pioneering work.

Stephen Hawking essentially normalised disability; proving, as Professor Paul Shellard put it, 'that there is no boundary to human endeavour'.[6] Stephen's indomitable spirit and tenacity can be summed up in his own words: 'My advice to other disabled people would be, concentrate on things your disability doesn't prevent you from doing well, and don't regret the things it interferes with. Don't be disabled in spirit, as well as physically.'[7] You can't really argue with that.

Pressure Is a Black Hole

Pressure and black holes are alike in the sense that they are both intangible yet powerful forces and Stephen Hawking can be considered as having expertise in both areas. As his profile grew, so did the pressure on Stephen to deliver and also manage his disability; his response to both offers us an excellent example of how pressure can be not only survivable but can be channelled into better efficacy and outcomes.

Win 1: 'Look up at the stars'[8]

Stephen's own words here serve as our first well-being win, though perhaps our interpretation of this will be somewhat less literal than he intended. Looking up to the stars can serve as a reminder to consider the bigger picture and context of our work – what called us to the profession and drives us. Teaching is loaded with high-pressure situations: inspections, performance management, student outcomes not to mention the core business of safeguarding the children who are entrusted to us. It's so easy to lose sight of our priorities – at which point reminding ourselves of the bigger picture can be extremely helpful.

In the midst of a high-pressure situation such as an Ofsted inspection, try to take a minute in order to recognise it as the ephemeral and transient process it is. While an experience like Ofsted can have longer-term consequences, it is important to try to avoid catastrophising or placing too much emphasis on your individual role or contribution. Always remember why we work tirelessly for our learners – to give students the best life chances possible – and that our everyday practice should therefore be more than sufficient to satisfy any short-term pressure. It's helpful to remember that organisations such as Ofsted are regulatory bodies, not what drives us and our schools. Howsoever idealistic that sounds, it's worth keeping in mind (and saying aloud whenever needed!)

De-escalate high-pressure situations by:

▶ taking a step back from the task at hand and taking a moment to connect it with the wider intent behind it (and, crucially, the intended impact on students)

▶ challenging intrusive or illogical thoughts such as 'I'm letting the school down' – writing these down can often help in recognising them thusly

▶ allowing yourself regular brain breaks to ensure that you don't lose sight of the bigger picture

▶ prioritising to ensure that the work you're doing is required at that time and schedule anything that can wait!

WELL-BEING WIN 4: STEPHEN HAWKING AND PRESSURE

Looking up at the stars also encourages us to take a macro view of a micro situation, by which I mean looking at any issue on the biggest scale possible. For example, an issue within your class with engagement is likely to be an issue in other classes within your school, your local authority and probably the country too. However 'big' it feels to you, it's likely to be part of a broader context. It can be extremely comforting to remind yourself of this when that which is truly micro feels macro in terms of your daily life. At any given point it's important to stop, pause and channel Stephen Hawking by looking up at the bigger picture on the largest possible scale you can imagine.

Big picture thinking entails:

- taking a long-term view of impact
- accepting short-term pain for long-term gain
- prioritising strategy over that which is operational
- de-personalising your input into a strategy in favour of the wider aim
- thinking in 'idea' terms then scaling back in-line with resources.

Win 2: 'Intelligence is the ability to adapt'[9]

One of the many joyous aspects of the profession is that it never stands still: change and challenge are absolutely inevitable. Applying Stephen Hawking's definition of intelligence necessitates that we adapt accordingly – and perhaps this is where the true key to longevity in our great profession lies. Whether from external or internal directives, the only certainty is uncertainty – in other words, change is inevitable.

Sometimes it isn't about our ability to adapt, but actually our willingness. As teachers we often find that new initiatives aren't actually new – it's easy to become cynical – especially when initiatives are influenced by the changing political landscape which can inform the agenda of regulatory bodies. With that said, change for the sake of change should be avoided at all costs. I would hope that the culture and ethos within your schools is conducive to appropriate professional challenge – the sort where you can find out what (or who) is driving change within schools (and crucially, why?)

Get on board with change by:

- doing your research – how have other schools implemented the same change and what has worked well? What strategies didn't deliver?

- taking the time to contextualise directives – what factors will affect the success of this change which are specific to your school? How can you mitigate against these?
- exploring the intended impact of change of learners – it's often necessary for us to remind each other who the most important stakeholders are in our schools
- getting evidence-informed – what research is there around this change? Consult the Educational Endowment Foundation (EEF) and any other published empirical evidence you can access

Getting on board with change is not:

- accepting all new initiatives without considering how suitable it is for your students or context
- buying into fads
- implementing change with no clear intent or intended outcome
- introducing something 'extra' if the relevant foundation is not yet secure.

Ultimately Stephen Hawking's definition of intelligence can be extremely helpful in managing our day-to-day well-being – as teachers and schools we should always be looking to do things better wherever possible. The work of Dylan Wiliam resonates here: 'Every teacher needs to improve, not because they are not good enough, but because they can be even better.'[10] In other words, we should seek to create a culture in which all practitioners seek to 'improve not prove'. Therefore, we should seek to prioritise small, measurable actions which improve practice, rather than dedicating too much time seeking validation or acknowledgement that we're 'good enough' and instead focus on doing things a little better. Ironic really, given that Stephen was a master of proving – taking theory to theorem – that we should take inspiration from him in order to give ourselves permission to step away from proving ourselves.

Ways to improve not prove

- Use data to diagnose what is working well – rather than to just identify developmental areas.
- Refer to areas you're curious about rather than 'lines of enquiry'.
- Try not to be defensive about an issue you are having – ask for support and strategies (and act on them!)
- Be proactive and open about things you want to work on – and own them!

▶ Challenge the narrative that expert practitioners cannot develop their classroom practice further – because everyone can actually be better at something.

If this ethos was adopted profession-wide, can you imagine the impact on our collective mindsets and attitudes towards quality-assurance and monitoring and evaluation? How liberated (and empowered) would we feel if monitoring was actually a genuine commitment to improve an area of practice, rather than a box to tick on Blue Sky (or similar)? By changing our attitudes to change, this really could amount to a seismic change for the profession and by proxy for our learners.

Win 3: 'Life would be tragic if it weren't funny'[11]

Classical theatre conventions tell us that comedy and tragedy are indeed polarised mediums and the hand that Stephen Hawking had been dealt in life certainly qualifies him to comment on both. Undoubtedly something which saved Stephen from being considered a victim was the quality of his work, but also his proclivity for humour.

Stephen never lost his ability to laugh at himself as his litany of cameo appearances attest: *Big Bang Theory*, *The Simpsons* and *Futurama* are just a few TV shows in which he starred.[12] Of course there is a fine line between maintaining a sense of humour and becoming a punchline – which he executed expertly.

In terms of the well-being within your department, school or trust, do not underestimate the role of levity and humour in building a team and contributing to an ethos in which joy is permitted and enabled. That isn't to say that you should seek to entertain stakeholders or undermine your professional credibility by acting the fool but all schools are places where joy should be front and centre – especially as so few students innately love learning – and together with other extrinsic motivators, joy can really ease the well-being of all stakeholders.

Laughter is an extremely effective antidote to stress and pressure. Drawing on the science (which Stephen would absolutely advocate), laughter releases endorphins, stress hormones and increases our ability to ingest higher levels of oxygen-rich air.[13] It can also boost your immune system and reduce your blood pressure. Promoting humour and joy in your daily practice is no joke – and one which has the capacity to reap huge well-being wins.[14]

Joy is a necessary component in the profession, regardless of your role. Joy, rigour and high educational standards can absolutely co-exist – but this is nuanced work which needs to be built upon a foundation of discipline, routines and safety. Often, it's a natural by-product of working with children, some classes and circumstances spark joy naturally – and sometimes we need to pull a Hawking in order to create and engineer more enjoyment.

Perhaps the place to start in assessing how much joy there is in your daily practice is to explicitly audit it. Where are you experiencing and facilitating joy? How can this be further exploited to create a sense of belonging? Stephen Hawking might have favoured finding the value of X but we can absolutely quantify the value of joy.

Some questions to consider

- How high profile and visible are rewards in your lessons/classroom/school?
- Where/how does joy feature in your school's values or mission statement?
- How are trips and other enrichment opportunities conducive to staff and students building relationships and shared experiences?
- How often does the whole school community come together for celebrations?
- How is the contribution of staff rewarded and acknowledged?
- How much positive feedback do parents receive? How frequently?

Similarly, the facilitation of joy needn't be defined as laughter – it can also be considered as dedication to making others feel good. Possible ways for school leaders to do this without creating additional workload could include:

- regular staff star of the week nominations and recognition in staff briefing
- building in time to allow students to thank a member of staff – providing the stationery and delivery service if necessary
- ensuring that positive feedback is shared with all stakeholders
- carefully considering whether the Performance Management/Monitoring Evaluation and Review approach is meaningfully executed (see also Win 2!)

Joy in schools is not:

- 'a fun lesson'
- an opportunity to lower expectations
- enabling unprofessional relationship/interactions between staff or between staff and students
- compromising an ambitious curriculum.

It's also incredibly powerful to actively discuss joy in school forums and to pursue this as you would other indicators of a school's culture and ethos. Placing joy onto the

WELL-BEING WIN 4: STEPHEN HAWKING AND PRESSURE

seemingly endless list of areas to improve might feel like a futile endeavour, but the outcome may just surprise (or amuse) you.

Overall, Stephen Hawking was a man whose work spoke for itself. As an academic who fought and sacrificed in order to receive the recognition he deserved, there is no finer example of how disability needn't define an individual. Where others saw obstacles, Stephen saw opportunity and when motor neurone disease limited him physically, Stephen reminded the world of the limitless power of the mind. Professor Stephen Hawking is rightly remembered as a paragon of perseverance in the face of unimaginable pressure, to whom we are still incredibly indebted.

Look out for the Stephen Hawking archetype in your school/trust/network and watch how they:

- appear to effortlessly manage high-pressured situations – without a compromise in outcome
- are relentlessly positive especially in the face of adversity
- seldom complain about things they can't control
- are resolutely solution-focused – and are universally lauded for this
- discharge their duties as though they have nothing to prove.

Conversation Starters

Be a force for good and allay pressure by talking through the following

How can our school recruit and support more staff with disabilities?

What positive representation can we offer of disability?

What is the bigger aim of this initiative/who are we doing this for?

How can we make this better for our disadvantaged/SEND/previously low attaining students?

Case Study

Mr D is a recently appointed Head of Creative Faculty at a large academy in Manchester However, his Hawking era heralded straight after he received internal promotion in his previous school as Head of House and Lead for Well-being and Relationships. While during the (successful) interview Mr D had powered through in the knowledge that he was unwell, it's fair to say that he was staggered to receive a diagnosis of stage 3 bowel cancer within days.

Therefore, when September came around and Mr D was undergoing chemotherapy rather than delivering new intake assemblies, he was devastated. As well as dealing with uncharted health territory there was the added pressure of missing the beginning of the academic year. Health-wise, Mr D was thrilled to learn that his cancer was localised – however the thought that his new role was in freefall loomed large.

One term later, happily Mr D was well enough to return to school but the pressure was immense – he was aware that people would be looking to him to see if he was still up to his actual job, let alone his new role. Mr D also put pressure on himself, keen to distract himself from his illness and aware that his ability to perform (in every sense) at school would be the ultimate corollary that he was well again. In addition, Mr D now had a stoma bag to manage which also brought unique pressures – not least of all on a practical level in an already time-starved school day.

In true Hawking style Mr D used his illness and subsequent disability to alter his perspective – throwing himself into his new role by refusing to 'sweat the small stuff', setting himself achievable goals and seeking solace in the opportunity to be creative. One of his favourite aspects of his new role was the opportunity to break new ground in a role that hadn't existed before, which proved to be an unexpected means of allaying pressure.

Like Stephen Hawking, Mr D used humour to alleviate pressure – actively looking to embrace and facilitate joy (and using his new role as an excellent excuse to do so!) The new role ultimately offered an infusion of normality which proved to be the perfect antidote to the uncertainty of his illness and subsequent treatment; he was grateful for his new role as this prevented him from wallowing in his situation. Returning to work in his new role had served as a goal to work towards during chemotherapy and the gratitude this facilitated served as a real well-being win – albeit a most unwelcome one.

Final Takeaway

You don't have to understand the theory of everything in order to make an impact, channel Stephen Hawking in order to keep pressure and performance relative.

Notes

1 Penrose, R. (2018) Mind Over Matter: Stephen Hawking's Obituary. *The Guardian*, 14 March. Available at www.theguardian.com/science/2018/mar/14/stephen-hawking-obituary (accessed 22 July 2023).

2   Ibid.
3   Volkas, R. (2018) A Brief History of Hawking's Scientific Legacy. *Pursuit*, 20 March. Available at https://www.mndassociation.org/media/latest-news/professor-stephen-hawking-one-year (accessed 15 July 2023).
4   Penrose, Mind Over Matter.
5   Ibid.
6   Gallagher, J. (2018) Hawking: Did He Change Views on Disability? *BBC*, 14 March. Available at www.bbc.co.uk/news/health-43399921 (accessed 21 July 2023).
7   Dreifus, C. (2011) Life and the Cosmos, Word by Painstaking Word. *New York Times*, 9 May. Available at www.nytimes.com/2011/05/10/science/10hawking.html (accessed 19 July 2023).
8   McGowan, M (2018) 'Remember to Look Up at the Stars': The Best Stephen Hawking Quotes. *The Guardian*, 14 March. Available at www.theguardian.com/science/2018/mar/14/best-stephen-hawking-quotes-quotations (accessed 19 July 2023).
9   Ibid.
10 Wiliam, D. (2023) Teacher Quality: What It Is, Why It Matters, and How to Get More of It. *Impact (Part of My College)*, 31 January. Available at https://my.chartered.college/impact_article/teacher-quality-what-it-is-why-it-matters-and-how-to-get-more-of-it/ (accessed 1 June 2023).
11 McGowan, 'Remember to Look Up at the Stars'.
12 Penrose, Mind Over Matter.
13 Powell, A. (2023) A Laugh a Day Keeps the Doctor Away? *The Harvard Gazette*, 25 January. Available at https://news.harvard.edu/gazette/story/2023/01/a-laugh-a-day-keeps-the-doctor-away/ (accessed 3 March 2023).
14 Ibid.

WELL-BEING WIN 5

A Chapter by Tracey

Taylor Swift and Workload

[noun] An individual who upholds boundaries and still achieves greatness.

I aspire to be like the deputy head; he is a real Taylor Swift.

WELL-BEING WIN 5: TAYLOR SWIFT AND WORKLOAD

Taylor Swift knows more than a thing or two about withstanding pressure, owning success and generally sticking it to the patriarchy. Having transcended genres and expectations alike, Taylor has blossomed into an undeniable icon as a writer, performer and social commentator and is widely considered to be a key cultural figure, the epitome of talent and an unapologetic champion for women.

Born in 1989 in West Reading, Pennsylvania as the eldest of two siblings, Swift signed her first music deal aged fourteen – already making history as Sony's youngest ever signing.[1] It's safe to say that this paid off (in every sense!) as Taylor has proven herself to be a prolific writer and artist. Throughout her career, she has admirably fought a public fight against being objectified within an image-driven industry, not to mention the inherent sexism at the root of the endless focus on her (not really that exciting) love life, as opposed to her actual music and talent. It is perhaps her determination not to be viewed through the male gaze which best defines her, together with her undeniable talent.

In 2006, Taylor's first album coincided with the advent of social media. This was an *era* in which women were widely objectified and sexualised by the mainstream media irrespective of age – and not afforded a right to reply, given that there wasn't really a platform from which celebrities could speak directly and freely. From the onset Taylor rallied against this, striving for her talent and writing to be recognised, as opposed to the preferred pervasive narrative of the era in which women's achievements were reduced to copy focused on weight, outfits and boyfriends. All of which feels oh so pre Me-Too.

Since her debut release, Taylor has gone on to accomplish stratospheric greatness, racking up awards and acclaim in equal measure, rightfully earning herself a place in history as a true twenty-first-century trailblazer and talent. She has also accrued a hardcore fanbase which serves as an inspiration, inciting devotion from the so-called Swifties. Taylor heralded a new world *era* for artists everywhere, through her symbiotic interaction with fans, and her innate ability to own and celebrate her own narrative.

However, amongst all her success, it is arguably Taylor Swift's quest for wider justice which will come to define her legacy. Case in point: in 2017 David Mueller, a former DJ, sued Taylor for wrongful dismissal. In response Taylor counter-sued for sexual assault. While we can't know for certain whether she would have ever publicly addressed the real reasons why Mueller was dismissed had he not initiated legal action, suffice to say that Taylor is well aware of her platform and acts with intent as a result. The court subsequently ruled that she was indeed the victim of sexual assault and awarded her a symbolic $1 in damages, which Taylor intended to serve as a message to assault victims everywhere. Slay.[2]

Similarly, Taylor has fought for autonomy within her career: when Scooter Braun infamously sold the master rights to Taylor's first six albums, she simply set about recording her own version rendering the previous versions contraband for true Swifties.[3] This broader issue of intellectual ownership clearly transcends the transactional nature of such a deal – once again Taylor Swift reminds us that it's okay to fight for what is rightfully ours, and also that true autonomy has a price.

Workload Is Not Your Lover

Teacher workload is often cited as a key reason why teachers leave the profession[4], and remains a challenge on a more systematic level. A key factor in this is a seeming lack of time (*see also Well-being Win 7 – Dolly Parton*) as working until *Midnight* is simply not conducive to optimum well-being. Simply put, there is no magic bullet when it comes to teacher workload – it's important work with high stakes accountability, but that isn't to say that we need to accept that teaching is a job that will never feel finished, nor that we should be expected to subjugate ourselves in pursuit of excellence. Over to Swifty: despite never running a school residential nor being taken for cover in her only free of the day, there is still plenty that we can learn from Taylor's career, achievements and lyrics to empower teachers to manage our ever-expanding workloads.

Win 1: Shake It Off![5]

As a profession we are *so* resilient, and just as Taylor Swift has adopted this mantra to address negative feedback, we too can use this as a means of creating the longer-term longevity the job needs. At the end of each day there are myriad workload-related issues which we could take home with us along with our lanyards, ranging from minor annoyances such as a jammed photocopier to serious safeguarding issues. Though it's easier said than done, we need to strategise and prioritise what we take home with us literally as well as figuratively, and if it's not urgent – shake it off.

While unpacking your day may be helpful in the short term, it's also a good idea to put a limit on the time you spend talking shop at home. No matter how doubtlessly dedicated you are to your job, you simply cannot allow it to dominate all your time out of school – because it so easily could – with a clear cost to your well-being.

In terms of serious safeguarding issues, the need to offload and talk situations through (confidentially and operating within the confines of your school's safeguarding systems and structures) is paramount and as such needs to be built into your work day. For less time-sensitive work you need to strategise what comes home with you. As a general rule if it can wait – let it. In other words, prioritise according to which tasks are required first. For example, clearing email at the end of each working day is one task I will do in the evening, prioritising as I go. This is the part of the day where I will complete my to-do list for the following day. For me, this is a task I can complete when I'm tired and gives me a sense that I am in control of my own workload (howsoever

WELL-BEING WIN 5: TAYLOR SWIFT AND WORKLOAD

illusionary and ephemeral!) I've also learnt that I am at my most efficient in the morning and I earmark a 'power hour' from 8:00 the following morning where I take great pride in blitzing my list. Clearly, we all reach our peak energy at different points, and a key part of this well-being win is shaking off the idea that you have to work at times which suit others, as opposed to making your workload work for you.

Another strand to this is accepting that you can never fully feel on top of your workload. Because you absolutely can't. It's essential to shake off the quest for perfection in favour of prioritising impact because the academic year truly is a marathon and not a sprint! So pace yourself, acknowledge your limitations and shake off as much as you need.

Other things to shake off

- Over-prioritising an observation lesson
- Negative feedback which is a by-product of having high expectations
- General Moodhoovers and cynicism
- Chasing perfectionism

Win 2: Look What You Made Me Do[6]

Teaching can sometimes feel like a battle between what we'd like to and what we *have* to do. For example if you give me a creative task, I will absolutely prioritise this over marking, admin or anything which feels like ticking a box. If our jobs were solely about interacting with students I can only imagine how short our collective to-do lists would be. Interacting with students is what brought us here; it's the thing that gets us out of bed in the morning. Ultimately, it's the reason we give so much of our hearts and souls to a job which in so many ways does not fit into the time we're given to do it.

It's easy to forget that we do have some autonomy as individual teachers and while this varies from school to school, our approach to managing workload and prioritising really is down to us – possibly more than we assume.

Prioritising our workload according to the level of need (what needs to be done, as opposed to what we'd like to do) can be key to keeping overwhelm at bay. For example, early in my career I took great pleasure in creating very aesthetic resources; before long it became apparent that this was a futile endeavour and that my time would be better spent on tasks which had actual impact on students.

It also feels important to state that we don't *have* to agree to do everything. Much of getting the job done in schools is a result of goodwill: the end of term trips, residentials, school discos can only happen if staff are willing and prepared to facilitate these. While these are obviously important tasks which broaden students' horizons and build

WELL-BEING WIN 5: TAYLOR SWIFT AND WORKLOAD

their cultural capital, it's perhaps worth being discerning in how much you volunteer for – and tempering this against the tasks you actually need to do.

As teachers it's often assumed that that we will say yes to any request made of us – after all we're public servants who change lives – but we are more likely to perform more effectively if we also hold our boundaries; in doing so we may need to say no with the same conviction as we typically say yes.

Nice(r) ways to say no

- Refer to capacity as opposed to time – 'I'm sorry, I don't have capacity to take this on' lands differently compared to 'I really don't have the time'.
- Asking 'Does the impact of this warrant the time investment?'
- 'I'd love to be able to help but I am currently over-committed.'
- 'If this can wait until the summer term, I'd be happy to look at it then.'
- 'If I pick up X, this will affect the time I have dedicated to Y; which would you like me to prioritise?'

It's also worth remembering that doing ten tasks badly isn't any better than doing three really well – or even worse six tasks which need to be unpicked because they contained errors/typos/inaccuracies, all of which were a result of completing too much at one time.

Insist on boundaries à la Swift by:

- setting a work curfew and sticking to it
- leaving on time at least once a week (mine is a Friday, but you do you)
- treating everyone's time as precious (including and especially yours)
- using your job title to depersonalise conversations: 'As Head of Year 7, does this need my input?'

Win 3: Wildest Dreams[7]

As teachers, our wildest dreams may differ from those of Taylor Swift – for a start she can attend a dentist appointment in term time and likely can use the toilet whenever she likes. In the case of teachers the dream is to manage our careers with Swift-esque efficacy without completely sacrificing our souls and joy in the process. I refer to this as a dream as my experience is that this is still something teachers, though entitled to such, are still working towards (myself included).

WELL-BEING WIN 5: TAYLOR SWIFT AND WORKLOAD

Some schools tackle workload with a committee or working party or ask for staff to complete an audit or survey about their own well-being – though well intentioned, this can ironically take capacity and add to staff workload. Which isn't to say that we as teachers should not enable such activities to take place, but that we need to be realistic about our own capacity – budget this and commit accordingly.

One such area is that of communication. We've already touched on how email is an area which can trigger teachers. The immediacy of email can be extremely helpful in enabling us to work efficiently, but it can also allow direct contact to us at a time which is convenient to the sender, and not necessarily the recipient. Many schools have policies where email signatures state that it is an expectation that email is responded to at a convenient time whereas others have a blanket ban on sending emails outside of working hours. Certainly, any policy which flags email as a potential well-being trigger is a strategy to be encouraged, but policy and practice centred around workload will only create impact if it is enacted and enabled – usually by senior leaders.

As teachers we need to remember that email is a tool to help you do your job; it is not your job per se. For some having your school emails on your phone is an absolute well-being win because it means nothing gets overlooked and this can give you a sense of being in control of your workload; for others (myself included) deleting the email app from your phone will liberate you from school having 24/7 contact – which is absolutely not a necessity in order for you to discharge your duties effectively!

Workload wins on an individual level

- ▶ Prioritise tasks with impact over ticking a box.
- ▶ Re-use and adapt existing resources and schemes of learning.
- ▶ Respond to email at a time which is convenient to you (and schedule send to model consideration for the working hours of others).

Workload wins on a whole-school level

- ▶ Complete an audit of staff's role and responsibilities to ensure that staff are not completing tasks for the sake of it.
- ▶ Allocate directed time with well-being in mind.
- ▶ Review the number of data captures – are these as streamlined and purposeful as possible?
- ▶ If you have capacity, look at how administrative tasks could be completed by non-teaching staff.
- ▶ Raise the profile of workload by including it at the heart of decision-making (and the School Improvement Plan if possible).

WELL-BEING WIN 5: TAYLOR SWIFT AND WORKLOAD

- Dedicate some INSET or CPD time to addressing workload issues.
- Create forums in which staff have access to feedback to senior leaders including the headteacher.

Ultimately, Taylor Swift reminds us of the importance of taking responsibility for our own workload, acting with intent and cultivating a long-term approach to success. In fighting to own her own voice and her steadfast refusal to be defined by anything other than her talent, Taylor certainly knows her worth *all too well*. In terms of the cultural zeitgeist, Taylor isn't just part of it, she has pretty much defined it.

Look out for the Swift-esque archetype in your school/trust network and watch how they:

- work intensely on a project and allow for respite before starting the next
- fight to ensure that they are adequately remunerated for their work
- wield power with intent because they are aware when people are watching
- are principle-driven and will take issue when this is challenged.

Case Study

Mrs T is an Assistant Headteacher in an 11–18 school in the North West who has pulled a Swift one so to speak in her leadership of Careers Information and Guidance (CIAG). Like many CIAG leads, Mrs T's practice was informed by the Gastby benchmarks, which specify eight indicators of effective career guidance. One of the key indicators centres around providing work experience for students.

However, Mrs T's school is located in a deprived area and the cohort struggled with the requisite social capital in order to secure meaningful placements. The placements were also incredibly difficult to quality-assure and historically this had caused issues around attendance/behaviour and safeguarding. Student feedback was also very polarised – it appeared that the most disadvantaged students had the worst experience. Mrs T was concerned that work experience was actually contributing to the very same social disadvantage she works so hard to address.

The issue of work experience was inextricably linked to well-being (and specifically workload) because many staff gained capacity from Year 10 being out of school. However, Mrs T recognised this is false economy due to the lack of impact on students and the workload generated for many staff (usually middle leaders) in the fallout from ineffective and/or unsuccessful placements. Not to mention the incredibly onerous work which went into organising the set-up of placements – the initial outlay of which was a significant time investment.

WELL-BEING WIN 5: TAYLOR SWIFT AND WORKLOAD

Thus Mrs T pulled a Swifty by thinking outside the box – she made a decision to prioritise impact on students over the validation of the Gastby benchmarks and relaunched work experience as a series of meaningful employer encounters which took place within school. These were measurable and truly impactful while also allowing students an insight into truly aspirational careers.

By placing the needs of children at the heart of decision-making and ensuring that this crucial work was undertaken well (as opposed to just 'done') Mrs T truly made an impact where it was needed most. Such was the success of Mrs T's approach to work experience she was invited to present her model to a city-wide forum during which she was praised for ensuring that the work, capacity and time dedicated to work experience truly benefited students. This approach was adopted by other schools who recognised that the historic (and altogether more conventional) approach to work experience was not the well-being win it appeared to be.

Mrs T was bold enough to contextualise the Gatsby benchmarks into what was appropriate for her school and students and, far from being penalised, she was recognised by the local authority who asked her to present at the city-wide careers event – an audience which mostly comprised headteachers, many of whom channelled Mrs T and Taylor Swift by adopting the same approach.

The real well-being win was for school staff and leaders who were able to ensure that the work they put into work experience really did *work* for their learners.

Conversation Starters

Pull a Swift one in terms of workload by having the following discussions

Is the time spent on this proportionate to the impact on students?

How can we give more capacity to this project?

What is the bigger aim of this initiative?

What is the priority here? What is the bigger aim behind this?

Final Takeaway

Taylor Swift is not defeated by workload and reminds us that we can be both acknowledged and well with clear boundaries. Swift energy is the key to your well-being era.

Notes

1. Britannica (2023) Taylor Swift. Available at www.britannica.com/biography/Taylor-Swift (accessed 12 July 2023).
2. Weaver, H. (2017) Taylor Swift Has Finally Been Sent the Symbolic Dollar She Won in Court. *Vanity Fair*, 7 December. Available at www.vanityfair.com/style/2017/12/former-dj-david-mueller-says-he-sent-taylor-swift-dollar-payment (accessed 17 June 2023).
3. Corscarelli, J. (2019) Taylor Swift Escalates Battle With Scooter Braun and Big Machine. *NY Times*, 15 November. Available at www.nytimes.com/2019/11/15/arts/music/taylor-swift-scooter-braun.html (accessed 17 June 2023).
4. TES (2022) TES Wellbeing Report. Available at www.tes.com/en-gb/for-schools/content/tes-wellbeing-report (accessed 31 August 2023).
5. Swift, T. (2014) Shake It Off. Los Angeles: Big Machine.
6. Swift, T. (2017) Look What You Made Me Do. New York: Big Machine.
7. Swift, T. (2015) Wildest Dreams. Los Angeles: Big Machine.

WELL-BEING WIN 6

A Chapter by Charlotte

Marcus Rashford and Compassion

[adjective]
The principle of demonstrating philanthropic, charitable and compassionate strategies.

That is a very Rashford well-being strategy

DOI: 10.4324/9781003409113-8

WELL-BEING WIN 6: MARCUS RASHFORD AND COMPASSION

Background

This chapter will focus on how we can access and harness the intention and compassion of Marcus Rashford. As teachers and leaders there is often a popular narrative that you need to be ruthless in order to have success. This is simply not accurate and therefore, we need to explore the role of emotional intelligence and empathy as main ingredients within education. How as practitioners we can look out for one another and help to empower and support when people are struggling. Schools should foster the ethos and culture of a family and a team. Also, in challenging times such as a cost of living crisis, a staggering rise in food banks and the issues of 'holiday hunger' as a result, Marcus Rashford's work is current, relevant and impactful and will be for a long time. He is more than a footballer and an example of going above and beyond – like many teachers today.

Marcus Rashford, born 31 October 1997 (so young!) in the Wythenshawe area of Manchester, is from a working-class family with four older siblings. His mother was a single parent who worked several jobs to ensure that her children were fed, often going without meals herself.[1]

He played for Manchester United from the age of seven and, prior to that, for Fletcher Moss Rangers from the age of just five. He has said to have learned tactics and football 'styles' from observing other iconic players at an incredibly young age. He has been compared to the likes of successful players such as Thierry Henry in relation to physicality and 'choreography' of the game. His England debut was in 2016 after playing for the England U16 squad in 2012.[2]

Everything about Marcus Rashford is admirable. He is a positive role model, particularly for young people, due to his talent, hard work and determination in football, representing his country and making us all proud! What really sets him apart, however, is his philanthropy and almost saintliness. His genuine want and desire to help others, particularly children, make him a true hero and one worth worshipping!

His philanthropic traits came to light in 2019 through his collaboration with Selfridges. He led the 'Box Campaign', which provided homeless people with a number of essential items over the Christmas period[3] and it was Marcus himself and his mother who handed out these boxes personally at homeless shelters. He also visited numerous children's homes in Saint Kitts and Nevis, his grandmother's home country. However, he became frustrated at the lack of impact that this seemed to have and he wanted to do more, so he persisted and in March 2020, following the announcement of the first lockdown, Marcus teamed up with food waste charity FareShare and aimed to support vulnerable families in the Greater Manchester area. His vision was to provide food for children who would usually access free school meals and attend breakfast clubs at school. The initiative quickly raised over £20 million and in June that year, Marcus revealed that the charity had been able to provide three million meals across the country, a figure that rapidly increased even more to four million in July.[4] Steadfastness, stubbornness and genuine care are key ingredients in contributing to these impressive figures.

His open letter to the government that summer had an instant impact. Marcus campaigned for and successfully ensured that children had access to food parcels during the summer holidays. His fight continued after he was appointed Member of the Order of the British Empire (MBE) in October that year and he carried on being the children's voice, fighting against inadequate food parcels and channelling holiday clubs and activities, as well as nutritious and sufficient food for families. His work continues and he has captured this within several of his own publications, both fiction and non-fiction books for children.[5] Everything he does is done with care and empathy. His own personal story has paved the way for his choices, as well as influenced his desire to help others in need.

It is his football talent that made him famous, well known and admired by many, but the real reason that I have opted to choose Marcus Rashford as one of our 'icons' in our well-being book for teachers is his compassion and sheer fortitude to make a difference. A humble fighter for social justice – that's why his story has made our book!

Win 1: 'Look what we can do when we work together'[6]

When discussing his preferred position in an article for *The Independent* in April 2020, Marcus stated:

> When you are on the left, you can create a lot more things on your own, giving that little bit more to the team. Whereas, when you are playing up front, sometimes you are isolated and need someone in midfield who can find passes for 90 minutes of the game, so you can disappear sometimes as a Number 9.[7]

This encapsulates Marcus Rashford's views and preferences on the pitch, but is also a mantra that he follows day to day and that we can all follow in our profession as teachers and leaders.

Undeniably the 'role' of a teacher has changed over time. Many naturally go above and beyond for all pupils and every day surpass themselves in ways that we do not think possible, due to the challenges and demands of the job. Many of us will relate to meeting rooms becoming in-house food banks and parcels delivered via the school minibus to families to support in difficult financial crises. Additional transition support is perhaps in place at many schools through enhanced summer schools and holiday activities and food, meaning that new Year 7 pupils are supported, due to the rise in mental health and safeguarding concerns across the country, but also globally too.

Academic rigour, ambition, drive and results are of course crucial. We know that this is needed as evidence and can open doors, but the moments that I reference above should remind us of the sense of togetherness and force that colleagues can bring when working effectively as a team and successfully, rather than against one another or in competition. Yes, there have been dark times, but look how we can sparkle as a community! To quote Marcus, during adversity, we as teachers and individuals within education have definitely played on the left, rather than in isolation!

Other ways in which we can successfully work together as team players

- Share good practice. If something works for you, don't be overprotective about it, but help one another. This can be within school, within a multi-academy company/trust or across different schools for peer-to-peer support.
- As a leader, involve all stakeholders in any decision making. This prevents the feeling of processes being 'done' to individuals, rather than 'with' them. Better results will form.
- Admit weaknesses and play to strengths. A successful team in any context thrives when this is in place. Leaders are not the best at everything – this is not humanly possible, sorry! – but draw on the experts around you in your team. Admit what you yourself are good at … and admit what you need help with. This is empowering for others to see.

Win 2: Social Education – Remember the Why

In the fast-paced nature of our role as educators we can sometimes become a little overwhelmed and lose sight of what is truly important. I am the first to say to colleagues that it is important to switch off, wind down and enjoy being present at home with family and friends. You may have heard yourself say so many times that we should not feel guilty for having a work-free weekend or a half-term holiday … but sometimes admittedly, we need reminding of our own advice! Rest is crucial but I can appreciate the guilt is also very real! I suppose this is only because we care so much though. By reminding ourselves of the *why* and intent behind what we do, it enables us to see with more clarity and to actually get whatever needs to be done *done*.

Overall, priorities can be a little mismatched when we are stressed in particular and we can spend time on tasks that really can afford to drop down a little lower on the 'To Do' list. Marcus had to act quickly with his initiative, prioritising what really needed to be done urgently, and look at where that led him.

Go back to the root and foundations of your vocation – advice for individuals new (and not so new!) to the profession

The amount of reading and advice on teaching and learning, pedagogy and educational leadership can be a little overwhelming. I look back and think that I would have greatly appreciated a concise list and key pearls of wisdom. Here are some of mine.

- Always model high standards for your staff and children and make no apology for this!
- It's difficult, but reflect on times of adversity and what we can take from it. There is often a greater focus on well-being during these periods and a sense of togetherness among schools and communities. Build on this.
- You're never on your own. Do draw on other people's strengths, expertise and contacts to get the results that you desire and to achieve the vision.
- We work with children and young people. To educate them and see them grow is the best gift. Sometimes the academic results may not turn out to be the best (we are humans working with other human beings after all!), but ensure that you look at how far they have come, their progress and development as an individual. Ok, this may not be 'measured' in the same way as performance tables are, but looking at the *bigger picture* reminds me of why it's the best job in the world.
- Sometimes we do have to take risks and make difficult decisions, but always come back to the *why*. If a decision will not benefit the children or have a negative impact then put simply, it's a 'no'.

Win 3: Empathy and Emotional Intelligence

I remember a friend and colleague saying to me once that when she first became a leader of a primary school she said to another colleague that she would have to instantly become more 'ruthless' and 'less kind', as this implied weakness. She would be viewed as a pushover and walked all over. Thankfully, another colleague corrected her – she apparently responded by looking at her, smiling and advising her (or rather instructing) that she should never lose who she is and certainly *never* lose her kindness.

I have been so lucky to work with people who are full of love and do teach and lead with heart, but have heard many horror stories about new teachers or new leaders trying to somehow 'reinvent' themselves and become pretty hard-faced and lose any sense of compassion. This genuinely troubles me – especially when we are trying to educate children and young people. I am not sure how it can be done without love!

WELL-BEING WIN 6: MARCUS RASHFORD AND COMPASSION

When first embarking in a leadership role, the initial aim and focus should be to sit down with every member of staff and to genuinely get to know them. Not just the fact that they teach in Year 1 and have been working at the school for three years, but to know *them,* as people. To know that they enjoy running, yoga, have three children and a dog, and to listen to their hopes and dreams. It sounds idealistic, but this makes people feel valued. It forms relationships, finds commonalities and similarities between colleagues. Such human connection and conversation are so vital and a key ingredient to winning hearts and minds – both among staff and children.

An individual level

- It sounds so obvious, but remember that we work with people, not robots! Complex feelings, situations and contexts mean that things are not always straightforward. Try not to pile on the pressure.
- Never be afraid of sharing thoughts and ideas, particularly if you have a vision and an initiative that will have an impact. Use the knowledge and expertise of colleagues or people that you know to support you.
- Work *with* others, not against.
- Never lose sight of the dream. If you have a good feeling about something and just know that it will make a difference, you will never regret trying.

A whole-school level

- Is pastoral care a priority above all? It needs to be!
- Do you know the children and their backgrounds? I mean, *truly* know? Can you relate and empathise? Are there successful 'handover' processes in place? For example, at primary and secondary school level between teachers and from school to school level if the child is transitioning?
- Is the PSHE curriculum bespoke to the school, ensuring that it fits the context and demographic appropriately?
- Is cultural capital something that you are looking to build on and enhance, ensuring that children are learning academically, but also personally and building memories and experiences?
- Is there a culture of compassion and togetherness? Any sign of 'negative clicks' just creates animosity and a bad atmosphere. Working together will achieve greatness.

WELL-BEING WIN 6: MARCUS RASHFORD AND COMPASSION

Look out for Rashford heroes/heroines in your school or trust and observe how they:

- really and truly care. They do the job with heart!
- can empathise with people, which forms relationships and gets positive results
- use the power of words to make a difference and draws on contacts that they know will help them to achieve their goals (excuse the football pun!)
- have a strong moral compass and do good … just because they *want* to do good!

Overall, because the above are fulfilled, they are happy and content – key ingredients for effective well-being

Case Study

Mr B has been teaching for nine years and in a senior leadership role for five years. For all of his career to date, he has worked in primary schools situated in disadvantaged and highly deprived areas. A huge part of his role as Assistant Headteacher has been Designated Safeguarding Lead for the past four years, which, although challenging, can also be incredibly rewarding. Often going above and beyond for the children in his care, he really has experienced some traumatic incidents, but never fails the children, acting as a champion to many.

Mr B claims that the most challenging of situations that he has come across are those where he and the safeguarding team have needed to step up incidents and escalate through social care when things haven't improved with families. There was one incident in particular where the team complained, so they met with the director for social care for the city because none of them were happy with progress and the safety of the family. Not being afraid to escalate and voice concerns is vital and ensures that the pupil-centred approach is constantly followed and embedded. This is something that he always comes back to.

A separate situation that highlights just how much he and other colleagues in a similar role give to families is the fact that they don't just support those who are still in their care and attendees of the school, but that they continue to do so long after they have left. He exemplified on this:

> One example would be a previous pupil who returned to us for support because they had lost both parents and knew that we would be there. We raised funds and donated to the family as well as offering a listening ear for the young man who would visit regularly. We do though have many who return to us for support as the ones in the community they trust.

WELL-BEING WIN 6: MARCUS RASHFORD AND COMPASSION

Showing compassion is about remembering that we see the tip of the iceberg and, despite having positive relationships with pupils and families, never fully understand their lives and experiences. Taking a step back during those most challenging situations, whether behaviour or safeguarding related, to consider actions rather than heated in-the-moment reactions helps to put things back into perspective when it could otherwise feel difficult to see a way forward.

Mr B goes on to say that:

> For many of our children, we are the only ones who truly advocate for their best interests and so it's really important to know the children and families well so that subtle changes can be identified and both children and families feel able to be open and honest. Always remembering that, no matter what we are being called, or how challenging a meeting may feel, it's not personal helps.

Taking care of ourselves is one of the hardest parts of being a leader and particularly a role such as Deputy Safeguarding Lead. Rightly so, safeguarding takes precedence over all else and this leads to many sleepless nights and school holidays spent worried about families. The biggest help he has found that works is by having a team approach. He admits to taking real strength from knowing that almost all decisions are made through discussions with the team and so, although the decision may ultimately rest with him in that position, being able to share the load and also challenge each other's thoughts really helps to ensure that the best decisions are made and the best outcomes are reached.

In true Marcus Rashford style:

> In the end, for the most difficult of cases, it's about remembering that the actions we take have the potential to impact on the whole of our most vulnerable children's lives – and a few sleepless nights are a price well worth paying to hopefully have a positive impact on their life-chances.

Start unapologetic conversations focused on compassion and kindness in your workplace through using the following tools

- When people speak to you, truly listen and be present. It is extremely difficult to stop your mind from drifting and thinking about the 'to do' list when busy, but offering someone your time can be the greatest gift – whether this be a pupil, parent/carer or colleague. Not only is it good for their well-being, but through giving and supporting, ours as educators or leaders can be enhanced too.
- When a pupil misbehaves there is often a story there, maybe a deep-rooted complex problem or a safeguarding issue and sometimes one that we can barely imagine, let alone relate to. By showing kindness and compassion we can truly win hearts

and minds and children are much more likely to engage. This reward only supports our own mental health and through the knowledge that we have made a difference, this means that our well-being and sense of worth flourishes.

Know you are 'more than a score'! In the data-driven culture that we sometimes find ourselves immersed in; this can be a healthy reminder to all.

Key Takeaway

Always remember the why. Remind yourself daily of the reasons you do this job and the impact you can make, but not at the detriment of your own mental well-being. The gains of the rewarding nature of the job do however far outweigh the challenges, but it is still important to look after ourselves too in the process.

Overall, the solution to a complex problem or equation often comes down to the roots and foundations, which are built on compassion.

Notes

1. Marcus Rashford official website (2023) About. Available at www.marcusrashfordofficial.com/about (accessed 4 November 2023).
2. Ibid.
3. Froggat, M. (2019) Why Rashford Needs Your Help This Christmas. *Manchester United*, 17 October. Available at www.manutd.com/en/news/detail/man-utd-striker-marcus-rashford-launches-in-the-box-christmas-campaign (accessed 4 November 2023).
4. FareShare Greater Manchester (2020) Marcus Rashford visits FareShare Greater Manchester's New Warehouse Which Will Help Feed Thousands More Children and Families in the Region. Available at https://fareshare.org.uk/news-media/press-releases/marcus-rashford-visits-fareshare-greater-manchesters-new-warehouse-which-will-help-feed-thousands-more-children-and-families-in-the-region/ (accessed 4 November 2023).
5. Ibid.
6. Coughlan, S. (2020) Marcus Rashford: Food Voucher U-turn After Footballer's Campaign. *BBC News*, 16 June. Available at www.bbc.co.uk/news/uk-53065806 (accessed 4 November 2023).
7. Connor, A. (2023) Marcus Rashford Is Back to His Devastating and Effervescent Best. *Breaking the Lines*, 31 January. Available at https://breakingthelines.com/player-analysis/marcus-rashford-is-back-to-his-devastating-and-effervescent-best/#:~:text=When%20discussing%20his%20favourite%20position,bit%20more%20to%20the%20team. (accessed 4 November 2023).

WELL-BEING WIN 7

A Chapter by Charlotte

Dolly Parton and Time Management

[noun] A person who can prioritise with ease, for the sake of their sanity.

'My colleague is so organised and efficient, not working all night. They're a true Dolly Parton.'

DOI: 10.4324/9781003409113-9

WELL-BEING WIN 7: DOLLY PARTON AND TIME MANAGEMENT

Background

We know that teaching is a vocation and that's what makes it so special. Due to this however, it can be overbearing and overwhelming at times, therefore using time effectively is so vital. We all have the same hours in a day and this chapter will explore how we can all choose wisely what we do with it, as well as how sometimes we need to make decisions and compromise and that as teachers and leaders in education we have more autonomy in terms of time than we first assume. This chapter focuses on the impetus and trajectory of Dolly Parton's legacy and career and how teachers can commandeer this in their own practice, particularly in utilising time effectively.

Unbelievably, Dolly Parton was born on 19 January 1946 and is widely known as a country-western singer-songwriter, but she is also an actress, philanthropist, businesswoman and writer, as well as the inspiration behind the one and only Dollywood theme park[1] – she is quite the entrepreneur!

Her well-known hits include '9 to 5', 'Islands in the Stream' and 'Jolene',[2] among many others, and she has won a total of eleven Grammy awards for her music. Dolly's tremendous success places her in a rare group of fewer than one hundred people who have received nominations for an Emmy, Grammy, Oscar and Tony Award. As her website captures, there are only sixteen people who have won all awards.[3] This highlights how influential she has been and still continues to be in the industries in which she works, as well as her range of effervescent artistic skills. There seems to be nothing that Dolly cannot turn her hand to!

She has also written several books, including children's stories and tales about her style and costume design, injecting nothing but joy, life, positivity and colour into the world. She has also collaborated with author James Patterson producing the novel *Run, Rose, Run*. Patterson described her as a 'gifted storyteller' and that 'every one of her songs is a story'.[4] Her ability to turn a creative hand to any project and to work so well with others highlights her character and likeable personality. She clearly takes people with her and encourages people to follow her dreams and, importantly, be a *part* of these dreams and ambitions. She is the epitome of tenacity and persistence.

Since a child growing up in Tennessee with an old can as a microphone,[5] she was destined to be a star and through nothing but a natural talent for show businesses and performing, sheer determination and hard work, she has become one of the world's most iconic women of all time, inspiring musical theatre, films, songs and performances all around the globe. Despite this and her universal fame however, it has not gone to her head and she remains grounded and humble. Her roots, her background and her faith remain important to her and truly shape and define who she has become.

When researching Dolly and exploring her life and work, it is difficult not to be inspired by her success. Her fame and her name alone have materialised into a huge iconic industry; her uniqueness and individual style, Dolly's charisma when performing and her philanthropy to other charities reflect a positive role model in many ways and a desire to want to entertain, as well as support others around the world.

What resonated with me the most, however, were her memoirs and what she calls 'Stories from the Front Porch'.[6] This is literally what it says on the tin, all about the family home's front porch, but more than this, it was a place of music, performance, quality family time and, overall, love and togetherness. This is surely something that we can lift from her and something totally, whole-heartedly applicable to a book focused on well-being and mental health balance.

Win 1: 9 to 5?[7]

I love Dolly's 9 to 5! Mostly because it can be interpreted in a number of ways and used in many different contexts, but for the sake of well-being and mental health (and for this chapter particularly), I consider this to be Dolly's sound advice relating to prioritising ourselves and our own growth and development. I believe, from experience, that if staff feel developed and a culture of reflection, improvement and aspiration is fostered, then individuals are happier and, as a result, more productive. I am uncertain of any science behind this approach, but have certainly witnessed this in the schools that I have been lucky enough to work in.

Dolly famously said: 'If you don't like the road you're walking, start paving another one.' Again, more witticism and pearls of wisdom from the Queen herself. If as educators we feel that we are no longer challenged, developed or learning ourselves then we need to embark on a different journey, a route of learning and self-reflection. This can be in the form of completing a specific course or qualification, pushing ourselves to the next stage in our career, for example, a middle leadership role or subject lead, or learning from other colleagues. The Education Endowment Report on Effective Professional Development exemplifies on an important point:

> Those who develop PD programmes must balance the desire to promote lasting and meaningful learning with the imperative to minimise the pressure they are placing on teacher time.[8]

The report and research epitomises a Dolly-esque viewpoint of valuing others, valuing learning and valuing *time*.

We have entered a profession dedicated to teaching and learning. We should model this ourselves, but as Dolly says, it is up to us to pave the way.

What other ways can we remain enthused and ambitious?

▶ Whether a senior leader or early career teacher, imposter syndrome is something that many of us can relate to. The sense of not feeling deserving of success or that we 'shouldn't really be here' must be abolished. Work hard, try your best and never stop dreaming! It keeps us driven and focused and as a result, performativity increases.

▶ CPD and general opportunities for all staff should always be on offer. Professional coaching is something that many teachers and leaders label as the most effective CPD received, particularly when perhaps new to leadership roles in particular. It can force individuals to reflect on their own practice, but also give tangible actions and 'take-aways' to implement, making you a better leader or educational practitioner generally. This is a cyclical approach because as you notice your own practice developing and enhancing, you then want to continue to set further targets and grow as a leader even more. A rolling snowballing effect!

▶ Show appreciation for others, whether this is appreciation for school leaders or for early career teachers, support staff, middle leaders. We should always show thanks for one another's hard work. This can retain staff and creates an open, transparent culture, as well as fostering a sense of ambition because people strive to perform. Overall, if people are praised, well-being is nurtured. It's not only pupils who thrive from such positivity!

Win 2: Lose the Toxicity

Toxic workplaces are just so dangerous and obviously no good for anyone's well-being. The term 'toxic' can mean a number of things, but key contributors are often professional jealousy and a lack of trust. This combination can drastically turn any workplace into one that is toxic and negative. If you feel this is something that you are unfortunately experiencing I would suggest that you simply raise concerns in a gracious way and most of all … look for another job. Life is too short! I have learned though over the years through working in education that being angry about things only impacts you. It can be all-consuming and, actually, this can be detrimental for your well-being. You are only punishing yourself. However, no one should ever take credit for other people's work and no individual should ever be ignored for making an impact. The power of being praised and thanked is one not to be under-estimated.

I think that collaboration is a key ingredient to a positive and toxic-proof workforce. If colleagues feel involved in decision-making and empowered to make and instigate change, this creates an atmosphere and culture of openness and effective communication. Who wouldn't want to work in that sort of place? If the talents of all are celebrated, then work does not feel like a chore. Let us champion collaborative work and team approaches within education. It is however, something that we try to instil in our children and young people after all, so why shouldn't we follow our own advice?

Ways that we can be heard

▶ Listen, be present and take everything in. Do your research and then bravely and courageously speak out in a professional forum, such as a staff meeting, leadership meeting or plant the seed with a trusted colleague.

▶ Put things in writing/email and evidence all successes in your performance management meetings, as part of the appraisal process. If you feel that you have to 'own' an idea or if you are concerned that others are taking credit for your initiative, you at least have some concrete proof of your creativity and ideas.

▶ Tell people what you want. This was arguably the best advice as I received when attending professional coaching sessions. This does not mean in an arrogant way, but unapologetically share your aims and ambitions with others. They just may be able to get you there!

▶ We should all champion one another. I am fortunate enough to be surrounded by inspiring leaders and it was one of those inspiring leaders whom I co-authored this book with! In a challenging profession, empowering others is a super-power!

Win 3: 'People look to Dolly for guidance, and she knows that' (Dolly's God-daughter, Miley Cyrus)[9]

As educationists we guide: whether we work one to one or lead small group interventions to push children to achieve within Maths or English, or maybe you guide as classroom teacher or form teacher, supporting young people through personal difficulties, providing them with pastoral help or academic drive and high standards. Maybe your role is in leadership and you guide your staff body, building the whole cultural picture of teaching and learning all together as a learning community. Working in a school should embody a feeling of guidance in different ways.

It still startles me how many fantastic teachers do not 'see the profession through', finding that they burn out after three years, or falling out of love with teaching because of the demands and lack of work/life balance they are experiencing. One of the most enjoyable parts of leadership can be supporting early qualified teachers and trainee teachers. Working with individuals from different backgrounds and walks of life is fascinating and listening to their stories and reasons for entering this profession is something that can be so interesting. More than this, however, it is important to nurture new professionals: ensure that we care for them, show support, but also ensure that they know the high expectations and demands of the role without of course causing stress and overwhelming people. This should include well-being as a foundation of many conversations and what these colleagues enjoy doing in their spare time. Being a guide and a small cog in the mechanics of keeping the teaching profession ticking over and working seamlessly, retaining the good worker and passionate colleagues, was an honour, but I also learned such a lot from them too, most of all to keep the passion and enthusiasm because you shine and radiate positivity when this is done.

Every single of us needs support; let's keep that going past the trainee years.

How we ensure that we guide one another

- Get to know colleagues (them as *individuals*, not just as colleagues).
- Encourage an in-house coaching approach so that staff, no matter how experienced, can be paired with others. This leads to not only celebrating the strengths of everyone, but also a non-threatening way of working on areas that people feel less confident in. This peer support can be hugely impactful.
- Leaders should have an 'open door policy' wherever possible, so that colleagues feel that they can approach and speak freely.

An individual level

- Self-evaluate. Do not simply wait for appraisal/performance management meetings.
- Reflect.
- Be forceful, but gracious and tell people what you want!
- Do not apologise for having drive and ambition. (If this means moving on for promotion then do not let this happen.)
- Have fun with it!

A whole-school level

- Development for all – does the school ensure that people are praised and thanked for their work?
- Do staff feel valued?
- What is the feedback process like?

WELL-BEING WIN 7: DOLLY PARTON AND TIME MANAGEMENT

▶ Do they have permission to be themselves, have fun, or are they dictated to and told to stay until a certain time, mark in a specific way? Lack of autonomy, not trusted, etc. These things cost valuable time and are therefore a *waste* of time.

Look how the Dolly-esque individuals do it

▶ Extroverted and confident – but never claim to know it all! It is a grounded confidence that helps them to achieve

▶ Do not compare themselves to others but celebrate being their own unique self

▶ Work hard, but make no apology for having fun and being *true* to themselves

▶ Use time wisely and therefore, do not feel overwhelmed by their 'To Do' list, as they know what to prioritise

▶ Own it! Have the ideas, but do not fall into the trap of not speaking out, not making suggestions. They will not be walked all over

▶ They are driven, hard-working and won't stop until they achieve the results/reward/success that they set out to grab!

Look out for the Dolly Parton archetype in your school/trust network and watch how they:

▶ are organised and efficient – no minutes are wasted!

▶ have a good and effective work-life balance

▶ manage to switch off and conserve energy for work

▶ are a 'doer' and not afraid of working hard.

Case Study

Mrs KS, a talented, hard-working and committed teacher, taught for eight years in an outstanding primary school. During her time there, she had many middle leadership roles and subject responsibilities. Positive feedback from colleagues, SLT, Ofsted and external subject inspections reaffirmed the impact that she has had on the children and the school, helping to sustain the 'outstanding' rating – not an easy task!

In January 2020 Mrs KS found out that she was expecting a baby. She and her family were ecstatic … but two months later, Covid hit and the world went into lockdown, meaning that she was quite literally ushered out of school under the new classification of 'vulnerable', not even able to assist with the key worker group provision in school.

WELL-BEING WIN 7: DOLLY PARTON AND TIME MANAGEMENT

Nonetheless, she remained positive, working from home, assisting with whatever she could and utilising the time wisely, despite feeling despondent at not being able to say goodbye to colleagues as well as the children in her care.

This level of resilience gave her a new strength, however. When she welcomed a beautiful baby into the world the following September, a new perspective was given. Time was a gift and slowly, as the world began to awaken and reopen again … and then closed … and opened(!) a simple recognition of the vitality and the precious nature of time arose.

Mrs KS deliberated over the decision to cut her hours down at work but when having her three-day working week approved, she felt an overwhelming sense of contentment. She still loved her job, that was clear, and she looked forward to seeing colleagues, spending time with the pupils again and having ownership of a class, but she was invigorated at having the time in the week with her baby boy and attending the baby classes and days out that she missed due to lockdown was a blessing.

This new found 'balance' in her life ensured that she was even more productive in school, no longer chatting during planning, preparation and assessment time (PPA), or spending endless hours printing off new resources and cutting out sorting cards. Instead, she was more focused and driven on what really worked for the children, not wasting time and energy unnecessarily. Her approach in relation to working smarter and more successfully helped her considerably with productivity and time wastage was avoided.

Teaching will never be a 9-5 job, but we can ensure that by telling people what you need, working hard and efficiently, great things can be achieved – in this case, a healthy work-life balance that suited individual goals and ambitions. Sometimes it is necessary to pause and use time in a different way. It made Mrs KS a better teacher and gave her a new appreciation for her role, as well as a restored balance and control of her career and life path. She is now a Key Stage 1 Lead, still working part time, but balancing parenthood with work-drive and ambition.

Talking Points

Raise the profile of effective time management in your school by instigating the following conversations with your colleagues

- Are there any unnecessary administrative tasks that are taking too much time and clouding productivity?
- Truthfully, are you procrastinating? Are you avoiding things and therefore, putting things off is leading to delay tactics and then stress?
- What helps you to wind down? Do you like to exercise after work? Do you switch off by reading a book (a non-work related book!)

Do you plan activities and things to do over the weekends and holidays that do not relate to work in order to reset and recharge? Perhaps you should!

Final Takeaway

In order to ensure that we have that appropriate balance and to avoid the 'taking and no giving' from employers, ensure that you work hard but also make no apology for turning phones off and logging out of emails. In particular, half-terms and holidays should not be utilised for 'catching up', but for relaxing and recuperation. Take time for YOU and do not say sorry for this! It leads to a more productive, organised, well-rounded and balanced worker … but also someone who has perspective and their priorities are right for them.

Notes

1. Dolly Parton official website (2023) About Dolly Parton. Available at https://dollyparton.com/about-dolly-parton (accessed 4 November 2023).
2. Dolly Parton official website (2023) Music. Available at https://dollyparton.com/life-and-career/music (accessed 4 November 2023).
3. Dolly Parton official website (2023) Awards and Milestones. Available at https://dollyparton.com/life-and-career/awards_milestones (accessed 4 November 2023).
4. Dolly Parton official website (2023) Books. Available at https://dollyparton.com/life-and-career/books/run-rose-run-novel-now-available (accessed 4November 2023).
5. Ibid.
6. Dolly Parton website, About Dolly Parton.
7. Parton, D. (1980) 9 to 5. Nashville: RCA.
8. Education Endowment (2021) Foundation Effective Professional Development Guidance Report. Available at https://eef-guidance-reports/effective-professional-development/EEF-Effective-Professional-Development-Guidance-Report.pdf?v=1699115417 (accessed 4 November 2023)
9. Najib, S. (2022) Dolly Parton Posts Tribute to Miley Cyrus on Her 30th Birthday: 'Can't Wait to Celebrate with You'. *People*, 23 November. Available at https://people.com/country/dolly-parton-posts-birthday-tribute-to-miley-cyrus-on-her-30th-birthday/#:~:text=%22People%20look%20to%20Dolly%20for,she%20leaves%20no%20one%20behind.%22 (accessed 4 November 2023).

WELL-BEING WIN 8

A Chapter by Charlotte

Joe Wicks and Positivity

[adjective] Used to describe someone or something that possesses effervescence, energy and positivity!

That is SUCH a Joe Wicks attitude.

WELL-BEING WIN 8: JOE WICKS AND POSITIVITY

Background

Joseph Trevor Wicks was born on 21 September 1985 in Epsom, Surrey. His father was a roofer and his mother, a social worker. Joe Wicks soon discovered a passion for sports and fitness during his school life and went on to pursue this further at St Mary's University in Twickenham, where he studied Sports Science. Following his graduation, he interestingly went on to at first become a teaching assistant, then decided to venture into a world of personal training, where doors were definitely opened for him.[1]

Fitness was his love and from planting the seed on social media – particularly videos on Instagram – Joe was able to encourage others to feel the same, attracting a huge number of followers in 2014, which continued to grow and currently stands at 4.5 million. His 'brand' of 'The Body Coach' has led to him publishing his books, the *Lean in 15* series,[2] which all focus on the importance and simplicity of a healthy, balanced diet and, more crucially, how this can be *sustained*. As well as this, he has written for several other publications, appeared on many television programmes and interviews, set up his own TV programme, and helped children (and adults) during lockdown to ensure that they kept moving and had *fun* with it. The ultimate achievement was that he received his MBE for such impactful work.[3] He then went on to raise millions of pounds for Children in Need. He is a Guinness World Record breaker, determined fitness fanatic, relatable individual, and true hero and icon.

At points in time where joy was difficult to find and individuals were discovering a new 'normal', in came Joe Wicks with his effervescence, humour, positivity ... and star jumps! Not only did he remind us all about the beauty and importance of movement and exercise, but he also taught us to find pleasure and laughter in the simplest of things.

He speaks with such positivity and joy, always making people smile. I think that this is a true gift. As someone who is interested in fitness and exercise, particularly running, I find him to be inspiring and hugely knowledgeable in his field, but most of all it is his humility and genuineness that makes him an icon from whom we can learn so much. He may be an expert in Sports Science, but he also reflects and prophesies with wisdom about achievement and success, in whatever way you may perceive this.

Win 1: 'I always had the voice inside my head telling me to keep going – keep going and people will eventually follow'[4]

Joe has enhanced his fame over the past few years, mainly due to his online presence with his work-outs. They were aimed at children initially who were missing out on their standard PE lessons during school closures in the COVID-19 pandemic. He became a household name in 2020 due to these.

Although his eight-minute work-outs of burpees, press-ups, squats and, a personal favourite, the kangaroo hops(!) helped us all to keep moving and exercise, it was his perseverance and resilience that many of us can lift and apply to our own practice. He, like most, had low days, times when lockdown engulfed him and resulted in feelings of negativity, but his focus was still to bring positivity, light and fun through the medium of YouTube and the Internet. It may have at first been aimed at children and young people, but as this initiative grew, more parents/carers, families and teachers were drawn into his work-outs, perhaps adding a different layer to the day and a way of breaking up the intense online learning. This was educating in a different way, through different means.

The fact that his online following soon grew to over four million people on Instagram alone highlights how his name and brand developed. His success as the Body Coach is remarkable and shows how he ultimately believed in what he was doing. He knew it was with the right intentions and eventually this would make people buy into his vision and values; therefore he was taking a lead and encouraging many in the process. When we believe in the *value* of a task or a role, we become inspired, elated and excited for what opportunities can unfold. This is Wicks-ism. His story wasn't a straightforward easy one; it was a journey on which he embarked upon with different twists in the road, but when he realised his true passion, success started to form.

Other ways and strategies that will help us to 'keep going'

▶ Don't give up and ultimately believe and *know* that you can do it. If you have a new idea or project that you are confident will have an impact, make improvements or shape your place of work for stakeholders, particularly if working with children, persevere and keep going.

▶ Imagine that end goal, think about how that sense of achievement will feel, and go and get it.

▶ Balance. Joe Wicks, although a fitness coach who is passionate about his field, does not work out and exercise every hour of the day. Resting ensures that we are prepared for the next challenges more effectively and can handle difficulties with much more clarity and vision.

Win 2: 'We need to be exercising for our mental health more than ever'[5]

We cannot deny that mental health appears to be at the top of every agenda – and rightly so! The recent years have impacted people's well-being more than ever. Joe explained in a BBC documentary, *Joe Wicks: Facing My Childhood,* how he was 'not ready for the wave of emotion and gratitude that came through' following the success of the work-out videos of 2020. He went on to say that 'one thing [he] never expected was that so many mums and dads who took part with their kids would start contacting [him]. Not about their physical health, but their mental health.'[6]

In the documentary, he opened up about how his own dad struggled with his mental health due to a drug problem and his mum suffered with obsessive compulsive disorder. With help and effective therapy both are well. Joe's dad is now clean and they now have a very positive relationship. Joe did not want to fall into that trap, so he explained how he discovered the gym and fitness, ensuring that he looked after himself physically, as this made him feel better. He soon realised that it was greater than just wanting to sustain a healthy weight and lifestyle and it was not enough to simply focus on 'being lean', but the balance of exercise and eating well led to a more positive mindset and more positive mental health overall. This had a cyclical effect, as by looking after your physical self you look after your mind and vice versa.

Speaking in another interview for the Happy Place Festival in 2021 he simply said that the main thing and incentive about healthy living and healthy eating is how it makes us feel. This is the motivating factor.[7]

When people ask about how many miles we should run a week or how many times we should exercise, there is no specific answer, nor is there a 'one size fits all' approach, as it has to suit our day-to-day lives, which can be extremely full and busy … but it is achievable. Too many times we hear colleagues say 'I don't have time', 'work gets in the way' or 'there are not enough hours in the day'. A particular pet hate is when colleagues in schools have said that they 'haven't had chance to have their lunch'. Please make time. We all have the ability to create some balance and should do for our own individual wellness. Exercise and eating well are paramount. Work hard, but make time for and invest in *you*.

Other ways to protect our mental health

We know what to eat and what to avoid and we understand the importance of exercise and the release of endorphins on the brain, but there are other ways too that we can protect our mental health.

- ▶ Exercise can be in many forms – through sports, running, gym, work-outs or classes, but it can also be a walk in the fresh air. This can be invaluable straight after work and help us to relax and wind down into the evening. It can also be a dance in the kitchen or anywhere in the house to be honest – multitasking at its best.

- ▶ Protecting our mental health may also appear in the form of 'putting up barriers', saying 'no' to some things to avoid that burn-out. This can also be empowering and vital for our sense of worth.

- Look through past goals and 'To Do' lists. Be grateful and proud of what you have achieved.
- Spend time with loved ones.

Win 3: 'You won't win every day. Just don't let a bad day … become a bad week. Wake up, reset and go again'[8]

We have all been there. A lesson which did not seem to go to plan – perhaps the pace wasn't quite right, those 'lightbulb moments' were not present, behaviour was unsettled (and that's just a staff INSET day!) In all seriousness, you know where I am coming from though, one of those days, or more often than not, just an hour or a moment that has just not gone to plan.

Feedback is so important, whatever our experience, but can hugely influence and shape new teachers particularly. It is absolutely paramount that feedback is always clear, positive (there is always something to comment on positively!) with clear actions that aim to develop practice. The way in which feedback is *conveyed* is so important. Comments can be so damaging and messages muddled. The power of words is something that is not ever to be undervalued.

Sometimes what we may label as a 'bad lesson' is not a bad lesson at all, but a negative *moment*: not even a 'snapshot' and certainly not one that should hold you back. Sometimes we have bad days, and we're not our best selves. Sometimes our colleagues have bad days and perhaps sometimes you may receive feedback that you have to smile and nod at, but internally you disagree with. Use this as a positive. It doesn't feel like it at the time, but it is actually a gift. Use it wisely.

Do not let negative moments define you. It does not mean that you have had a bad day, bad week, term, year or that you are no longer good at your job. We work with human beings and our job is complex – try to avoid piling on the pressure. The truth is that actually you may well be faced with many other similar moments or learning 'episodes', let's label them as, but the difference is that they no longer make the headlines because it's all about 'resetting' as Joe calls it.

The above quote from the man himself is referencing food, but actually I apply his philosophy to every day. The small 'failings' can indeed teach us a *lot*.

In summary, let us pause and think about the Body Coach mantras: Joe Wicks, an individual from Surrey, who grew up in a complex environment at times, faced turbulent family difficulties, but from this learned how crucial it is to take care of *you*. Although not always easy, the rewards of exercise and healthy eating can help to create and sustain some element of balance in life.

WELL-BEING WIN 8: JOE WICKS AND POSITIVITY

An individual level

▶ A phrase I often use is 'run the marathon, but eat the cake!' I have completed four marathons. I will never be fast, but love long distance running. I love the sense of achievement and discovering what our bodies are capable of (especially as someone who was definitely 'non-sporty' during her school years) and, as Joe says, how I feel after the run is incredible. I will never deny myself treats though and I think that applying this mantra of balance is important for work and life.

▶ It is so true when people say that there is nothing more important than your health. We are so guilty as teachers for being 'martyrs' at times and struggling on when we don't feel good. Looking after ourselves can prevent long-term issues. This includes eating three meals a day and not using 'break duty' as an excuse for not having lunch.

▶ Have professional goals – ambition is brilliant – but also have personal goals too. The two will complement one another. Be positive in achieving them.

▶ Keep going – if it's the start of a new term, perhaps a dark January after a rather indulgent Christmas period and you're just not feeling it, you *will*. Have hope. Think about your motivations and you will rise to the challenge.

A whole-school level

▶ Is well-being a focus across your workplace? Physical and mental and for *all*? Is exercise promoted and encouraged and in different forms to ensure suitability for everyone? I have known weekly HIIT training on a Friday evening, Zumba classes or staff football and running clubs. It must not be a hindrance though, but a help.

▶ Is time given to make sure that health and safety in school is not just referencing fire safety checks (obviously these are of course, vital), but do colleagues recognise that their own individual health, safety and wellness are considered within the whole school/trust development?

▶ Are there sufficient, appropriate and tailored professional development opportunities for staff to have goals and achieve them?

▶ Is there an 'open door' policy among leaders? Can staff honestly and openly speak to them about well-being – whether this be centred around health and exercise, or simply talking about something that is troubling them, holding them back or making them anxious?

▶ Are healthy habits modelled by leaders?

Look how Wicks wannabes do the following

- Influence the mood of the place of work – in a positive way.
- Balance work and exercise, ensuring that they look after themselves physically, leading to a calmer sense of well-being and positive mental health.
- They are not afraid to break the mould and try new things. They have faith in their vision and this confidence along with their efforts lead to success.
- They don't let one bad comment, bad experience, bad day or week define them. They have the 'bounce-back-ability' to rest and begin again.
- Don't stop at one challenge, but are always trying to better themselves and thinking about the next steps. They are never complacent.
- They work hard at everything that they do, but also recognise the importance of rest and recuperation – this after all, prevents injury and burn-out.

Look out for the Joe Wicks archetype in your school/trust network and watch how they:

- are genuine, kind and thoughtful people – and always have a smile, despite the tough days
- know and understand how important prioritising family is and how gaining and being present for such leads to an overall better work/life balance and well-being
- also know the importance of exercise on well-being and leave time for this – whether this is a run with friends or kitchen discos with their lovely family
- never forget the impact that they have on others, but are also humble with this. Occasionally reminding themselves about how far they have come gives them an added resilience, positivity and optimism. This leads to well-deserved great things.

Case Study

Ms H has been teaching languages at a secondary school in the Northwest since 2011 and in September 2020 became Head of Department. Previously she worked in recruitment, entering the teaching profession a little later on, which she believed helped her to gain transferable skills for her educational practice, but it also enabled her to prioritise and gain perspective. She is one of the most positive people you could ever wish to meet and a great mentor for everyone, but particularly teachers new to the profession. Everyone needs a Ms H in their life!

WELL-BEING WIN 8: JOE WICKS AND POSITIVITY

She believes that the most challenging time in her career was the transition from classroom teacher to middle leadership level. The step-up to the role of Head of Department was more of a big stride or leap than small step and, at times, felt quite overwhelming. As a parent too, it was a big decision as to whether to take on this challenge and she is grateful for support from friends and family that enabled this to be a smoother transition than it could have been. She admits that initially she 'was definitely unprepared for the workload and the challenges that came with leading a team'. Learning from others, particularly those who are more experienced, is valuable.

Ms H has a very busy personal life too. She says that 'it can be difficult at times to manage my work and home life; I am a single parent to two adorable, but energetic children!' Juggling things and regaining some sense of balance and control can pose difficulties; however, her positive and consistent 'glass half full' outlook helps massively. She is a huge advocate for not suffering in silence and always seeks help when needed. In her first year of middle leadership, she questioned herself a lot, feeling desperate to prove herself, but also needed guidance to get her where she needed to be. Working in a school where asking for support from other colleagues is encouraged is a blessing and leads to an openness and natural coaching approach within teams and across departments. She realised just how valuable this was and how prevalent this was at her school, as well as just how supportive and collaborative colleagues were at that time. This has helped in a new leadership role, particularly when feeling that no question was a silly one.

Her key to success, however, is that Ms H always strives to be optimistic in all areas of her life, not just work. Her philosophy is that 'If you're not [positive] it makes your time at work a lot harder. If you seek help there is always a solution. Ultimately only you can make the changes that will have a positive impact on your well-being.' Owning this is crucial; taking control, not being afraid to ask for help and support when needed and working with others is so important.

Ultimately, she is solution-focused and naturally driven. Ms H's view is that it's ok to have a moan and there may be a need to offload and have a professional 'therapy moment' now and again, with a trusted friend and colleague, but the reality is that if you don't make any attempts to change your productivity, work–life balance, classroom practice etc then don't continue to complain!

Talking Points

Encourage and model a positive approach at your school through trying the following methods

Always remain solution-focused. If something is bothering you or you want to instigate change, rather than focusing on what is 'wrong' and the negatives, make suggestions to create impact.

Learn from others, listen and respect the views of colleagues who have been teaching or leading a long time, and use and apply their good advice to your practice … but ultimately, stay true to yourself and your integrity.

Ensure that time is well spent, particularly family time. It is true that this brings contentment and then this positivity ripples into other aspects of our lives, including work.

Be open to learning, bettering yourself, but also view mistakes or challenges as learning opportunities that help us to grow and develop our pedagogical practice or general educational knowledge even further. We are all human and we will make mistakes from time to time. Be open and accepting of this, embrace the learning that comes with them and you will overall have a powerful growth mindset and great results … try it.

Final Takeaway

Gordon in his book *The Power of Positive Leadership* summarises positivity in a wonderful way:

> Sharing positive energy doesn't mean that you have to be a rah-rah leader and bounce off the walls. It means that from the heart you simply broadcast the love, passion, positivity, and purpose that you have for your team, organisation, and mission.[9]

A smile goes a long way, as does a kind word, positive attitude and supporting others, especially if someone is new to a school, new to a role or new to the profession. If each of us could contribute to a positive movement across our schools and an optimistic outlook, we probably would no longer need to have well-being on every agenda because it would grow and blossom. Let's support with a smile and, most of all, let's just be kind. It's an excellent starting point.

Notes

1. Surrey Live (2022) Where Did Joe Wicks Grow Up And How Did He Become A Success? 16 May. Available at www.getsurrey.co.uk/news/uk-world-news/joe-wicks-grow-up-how-23975327 (accessed 7 November 2023).
2. Ibid.
3. Ibid.
4. Wiseman, T. (2020) At Home with the Nation's Favourite PE Teacher. *Men's Health*, 9 April. Available at www.menshealth.com/uk/fitness/a32063119/joe-wicks-nations-pe-teacher/ (accessed 4th November 2023)

5. Wicks, J. (2023) Facing my Childhood. Available at https://www.youtube.com/watch?v=XoBeg2wccn8 (accessed 4 November 2023).
6. Ibid.
7. Wicks, J. (2023) The True Benefits of Exercise. Available at https://www.youtube.com/watch?v=CATfJT3HssQ (accessed 4 November 2023).
8. Ibid.
9. Gordon, J. (2017) *The Power of Positive Leadership*. Wiley (p. 23).

WELL-BEING WIN 9

A Chapter by Tracey

Tina Turner and Self-awareness

[verb] The act of commandeering self-awareness in order to accomplish the incredible.

'I am going to Tina Turner this inspection.'

DOI: 10.4324/9781003409113-11

Even after her death, Tina Turner remains an indelibly ubiquitous cornerstone of popular culture. As a performer, actress and survivor of domestic abuse, she epitomises resilience, re-invention and courage – all traits teachers possess and need. Tina Turner has come to symbolise strength – as a woman who fought hard to find her voice and seemingly didn't grow old, only more powerful. In being open about abuse and personal tragedy she owned her struggle and somehow did not become defined by it. Tina died in 2023 leaving the world with an enduring legacy (in addition to her music, a two-part HBO documentary, a musical and a biography).

Tina's home town of Nutbush, Tennessee was famously immortalised by song in the 1990s; however she was actually born Anna-Mae Bullock in November 1939 in nearby Brownsville. The youngest of three sisters, the young Anna-Mae had a nomadic upbringing, moving between family members initially because of World War II and later because of more complex familial dynamics.[1] It was when returning to live in St Louis after her grandmother's death that the sixteen-year-old Anna-Mae took her first tentative steps towards stardom.

Famously, it was here in St Louis that Anna-Mae first saw Ike Turner perform – a man who would come to shape the destiny of the young Miss Bullock in all ways imaginable. It's well documented that Anna-Mae commandeered an opportunity to sing with Ike's band as an impromptu audition and never looked back.[2] Tina's career is a tale of (at least) two halves, the first of which saw her perform as part of a duo with the (now-known-to-be-notorious) Ike Turner, who from 1962 was her husband as well as co-star. In these formative years a rebranded Tina Turner honed her distinctive vocal style, dance moves and unashamed sexuality like an absolute trailblazer.

Though Ike and Tina garnered critical acclaim and global stardom during their partnership releasing an astounding twenty-two studio albums, we know now that this success belied domestic abuse which was occurring on a staggering scale. By 1978 Tina had ended the marriage and had outed the abuse – courageous, fearless and ground-breaking in the context of the late 1970s.[3] Many critics assumed that without Ike's song writing, Tina would struggle to emulate the early success they had shared. Spoiler alert: she didn't.

When Tina emerged from her divorce like a phoenix from the ashes, it was as a phenomenal solo star who went on to sell more than one million records in her own right. This second act of her career was so seismic that it easily eclipsed the first. The term 'legend' is often banded around by popular culture, and can be attributed inanely. However, in the case of Tina Turner she has earned this title not just because of her commercial success or struggles but because of the indelible impact she has made on our collective cultural consciousness, which like Tina herself is beyond incredible.

Self-awareness which is River Deep and Mountain High[4]

So what's self-awareness got to do with it? Tina Turner is an inspirational example of how introspection and self-reflection (and love) can be extremely powerful tools for teachers, enabling us to become the best performing practitioners possible – and if we can accrue a fraction of Tina's longevity and tenacity in the process, wouldn't that be marvellous?

Win 1: The Best[5]

Arguably Tina Turner's most famous song offers us a masterclass in having high expectations – something for which we as teachers are renowned. Teaching is a unique profession because wanting to be considered 'the best' is not an inherently competitive aim, but rather an aspiration to bring about the *best* life chances possible for our students. The pursuit of optimum efficacy in teaching should not be confused with ego, as it is about equipping and enabling practitioners to best serve their students. However, high expectations in teaching are often at the cost of well-being – precise student feedback, planning for misconceptions and extension tasks all require time, capacity and commitment (not to mention compassion) within an already saturated workload. Being simply the best isn't actually that simple. How can we as teachers strive to be 'the best' without our personal well-being becoming collateral damage?

Teaching is similar to the entertainment industry (and perhaps society in general) in that the traits of extroverts are often held up as a model of success. Tina was a successful introvert in an industry which rewards extroverted traits. Whether you are an introvert or an extrovert, the better you understand where you sit on this spectrum, the better you will be able to perform.[6]

Introversion and extroversion has nothing to do with how confident you are (though is easily confused as thus). Rather it is simply a measure of where you get your energy. You may instinctively know whether you are innately introverted or extroverted, you may be an ambivert, or you have the ability to adapt according to specific circumstances.[7] Wherever you land on the spectrum, it is helpful to channel Tina and learn as much about yourself as possible in order to become the best practitioner you can. One possible avenue to explore is to complete diagnostics such as Myers Briggs[8] in order to better understand your preferences and triggers – ultimately enabling you to perform at a higher level of efficacy.

Moreover, it can also be helpful to share this knowledge within teams: understanding your colleagues on this level can help to build trust and improve communication as you work towards common goals. Understanding your introversion/extroversion preferences is key, because these preferences are inextricably linked with well-being.

For example as an extrovert if I work in isolation I quickly become unproductive and distracted; if left to escalate, this can impact on my workload and capacity and this is something I need to factor into how I approach deadlines and tasks, whereas in the same circumstances an introvert would thrive. Like in the case of Tina, this knowledge is powerful in terms of managing your role and workload.

In truth, there are massive benefits of both ways of working and regardless of your natural tendencies, you can draw on both styles in order to boost your own efficacy.

Hone your inner introvert

- Allow yourself thinking time in meetings.
- Listen more than you speak.
- Find out facts before you express an opinion.

Extrovert moves

- Put yourself forwards for tasks (especially if performative).
- Be decisive and clear about your intentions.
- Form purposeful relationships with others to amplify your impact.

Understanding your own energy sources will enable you to spend it accordingly, like money and time your energy is a currency and thus needs to be budgeted.

Where energy spends will pay off

- Creating high-quality resources which can be re-used
- Offering enrichment which broadens students' horizons
- Any work which raises standards on a large scale
- Implementing evidence-informed research

Where energy spends won't pay off

- Buying into faddy educational trends
- Prioritising marking over feedback
- Spending hours creating convoluted resources which could be replaced by a high-quality explanation
- Complicated planning documents which aren't looked at or revisited

Radiators and Drains

You may be familiar with the well-used analogy about radiators and drains. In teaching, who you surround yourself with matters. Radiators give energy and drains take it. There are lots of Drains in teaching (sometimes referred to as Energy Vampires or Moodhovers and often found in the staffroom). It's understandable because teaching is hard and challenging and this can breed cynicism. Take care to surround yourself with Radiators as much as possible; people who contribute, cheer for you and are relentlessly positive will be far better for your own mental state (more of this in the Joe Wicks chapter). Of course, it's impossible to avoid cynicism; it would be far easier to sit in the staff room and count down the days until half term but this wouldn't enable you to serve the students any better, nor preserve your own well-being. Ultimately, the better you know yourself, the better you will manage your own well-being.

Win 2: (Nutbush City) Limits[9]

We have mentioned boundaries already a lot; it's no coincidence that our icons are all prolific boundary holders and Tina Turner is absolutely no exception. Being a teacher requires dedication and commitment – it's a Mary-Poppins' bag which never ever stops. and without boundaries it can be completely relentless and potentially unmanageable. Therefore, however much you want to make a difference, limits and boundaries are key to managing your tasks and staying well in the process.

One easy way to enforce limits on your workload is to begin by communicating your intention to do so. The extent to which you're empowered to do this is likely to be determined by the culture in your school as well as how it's led. It is worth remembering that we are in the midst of a national recruitment crisis in the profession – for good reason. Schools cannot afford to be remiss or flippant about staff well-being nor to ignore staff's boundaries.

Whilst this sounds like an easy win, in reality the teaching profession presents us with challenges which can feel equally urgent and time sensitive and therefore prioritisation and self-awareness are key. For example, is it better for your well-being to switch off completely during the school holidays, or to set time aside to work and know that you are adequately prepared for the term which follows? After a decade and a half of leaving my marking in the car during school holidays, I've finally learnt (and accepted) that I am extremely productive in the first week of a new term and will complete it in a fraction of the time if tackled then. I likely knew this about myself years ago but never gave myself permission to work in this way because it seemed at odds with how everyone else worked. Using your knowledge of yourself to work more efficiently is a huge well-being win (and oh so Tina T too).

WELL-BEING WIN 9: TINA TURNER AND SELF-AWARENESS

Self-aware strategies to managing tasks in school holidays

▶ If you've chosen not to work, put on an out-of-office response to emails in order to be transparent and unapologetic about this choice.

▶ Consider where you work – are you likely to get something done in a morning if you're at school as opposed to at home? If so (and it's possible) work there!

▶ Set time aside and be strict about enforcing a time limit.

It's also worth being discerning about the sort of work you take home. Open-ended tasks are not necessarily the best to complete at home; tasks with a clear end point – such as marking – are going to serve your well-being far better. Similarly, if a task is important and requires strategic mapping and input from others, set time aside to complete this in school with input and in consultation with colleagues where appropriate.

Win 3: What's Love Got to Do With It?[10]

You can love your job and want a break from it, you can love your school and suggest ways for it to improve, you can love your students and not communicate with them over the Christmas holidays. Having passion and purpose in your role and wanting to stay well are not mutually exclusive, though in some quarters it can be assumed otherwise.

A side product of honouring your own boundaries and self-preservation is guilt – because in truth we could *always* do more. In order to truly preserve your well-being, it's not enough to simply enforce boundaries, you also have to do this unapologetically.

Banish boundary guilt by:

▶ remembering that protecting your own well-being isn't selfish – as it enables you better serve your students

▶ respecting the boundaries set by others in your workplace

▶ placing your boundary in the context of student impact, for example 'In order to have the energy to lead the residential, I am going to need to leave by 4pm tonight'

▶ challenging any emerging narrative that suggests staff who set boundaries are less committed to their classes.

So what's love got to do with teaching? Actually plenty, in fact sometimes *too much*. Furthermore, Tina's lyrics about 'second hand emotion' seem profoundly apt to describe what we as teachers experience in supporting our students – especially through the lens of pastoral support or safeguarding. We are often aware of awful experiences or circumstances our students are living in, and it can be extremely difficult not to absorb this and take these feelings home with us.

Teaching is considered a vocation for good reason. Teachers are often compassionate empaths and our passion is to safeguard our students through necessary (and indeed admirable) work, but the toll this takes on our mental health is well documented. Wherever possible we need to compartmentalise these issues in order to preserve our mental health; easier said than done but so very necessary. After all, what's love if you don't respect the game?

Separate emotion from practice by:

- rationally separating the things you can control from those you can't (and putting your energy into the things you can accordingly)
- reminding yourself that students spend a big chunk of their time in schools and keeping them safe and happy whilst in school will have a big impact on individual students in need
- being as present as you can at home (not checking email or perpetuating student contact)
- taking an objective view of the facts; list them if necessary and read them when you need an impartial reminder of the situation
- remembering (and then reminding yourself and anyone else who needs to hear it) that though it can feel incredibly emotionally intense and 'a work of heart' that it is nowhere near as personal as we might assume
- creating a professional persona and being very selective how much of your authentic self you share with students and colleagues (see also Well-being Win 1 – Beyoncé).

Many schools now subscribe to phone line-based support packages specifically to enable staff well-being; do consider accessing such services and agencies if you feel that you're too emotionally involved with a student in crisis (you can similarly raise this with your line manager, no matter how senior you are).

There are other instances where emotion can cloud our judgement: parental complaints, student outcomes and issues between staff can be all consuming, so honour your boundaries and compartmentalise as much as possible. You cannot possibly invest all your emotions into schools and remain mentally well, so by all means invest, but do so selectively.

Ultimately, Tina reminds us that obstacles can be opportunities, all adversity is temporary and that introversion and strutting are not mutually exclusive. Tina Turner will be forever remembered as an icon for her talent and tenacity.

Case Study

Ms M is a senior leader in the South East whose own professional career arc has mirrored Tina Turner's in several ways. Firstly, Ms M experienced complicated personal challenges not unlike Tina's and, in a similar way to Tina singing through her struggle, Ms M's performance at work (at that point as a middle leader) was unaffected – in fact school was a mainstay for Ms M in a time of personal upheaval.

Like Tina, Ms M was leaving personal crises behind where she used all that she had learnt about herself in order to garner more success in the workplace. As a confirmed introvert Ms M is a master of self-reflection and has accessed coaching in order to develop her confidence in the lead-up to applying for promotion.

After a decade in middle leadership and after accessing leadership coaching, Ms M realised that she had spent too much time overestimating others and underestimating herself. And though this opportunity coincided with the exact time at which the dust was settling from her personal crisis, Ms M felt emboldened to put herself forwards for an Assistant Headteacher post, realising that she was likely experienced and capable of the role.

As an introvert, an internal opportunity was initially daunting for Ms M; she felt instinctively that she tended to be overly self-conscious and felt that other staff underestimated her – ostensibly because she wasn't an overly performative leader. Leadership coaching enabled Ms M to recognise her own strengths and play to them accordingly.

As the middle leader with the best Progress 8 score in the school, Ms M decided to look at her own success from an objective point of view – starting by listing the impact she had had as well as all the previous posts held in preparation for interview. Though the voice of self-doubt hadn't completely gone away, Ms M was able to manage this in order to enable her to focus on the task in hand.

From the enlightened vantage point afforded by self-awareness, Ms M was able to recognise that in previous interviews she had overestimated more extroverted candidates simply because they presented as more confident. Through leadership coaching Ms M had recognised confidence and capability as two unrelated concepts.

On the day of the interview Ms M was quietly confident (yet *loudly* very clearly capable). To no one's (not even Ms M's) surprise she was offered the post. Ms M had channelled her self-awareness to pull off a Tina-esque career move. Since her appointment Ms M has made a huge impact on the school – this was recognised by Ofsted who visited within a month of her new role. This was an opportunity for Ms M to showcase her work and impact using many of the same tools she used in order to prepare for interview. Ms M had used her self-awareness as a superpower to amplify her voice and impact on young people proving that being simply the best isn't always the same as being simply the loudest.

Look out for the Tina Turner archetype in your school/trust network and watch how they:

- are resilient and respond positively to challenge
- allow their work to speak for itself with very little hype or hyperbole
- command the attention of others, seemingly with ease
- can be underestimated by others because they listen more than they speak.

Conversation Starters

Raise the profile of self-awareness in your school by instigating the following conversations with your colleagues

As an introvert/extrovert, in what context do you work best?

How do you complete creative/analytical/strategic tasks so quickly?

At what time of the day are you most efficient?

Why do we/I/the school spend so much time on ____? Could the time be better spent on_____?

Final Takeaway

In order to be simply the best, you first need to know yourself. Channel Tina T by introspecting and using this as ammunition to make big moves with your wellness intact.

Notes

1. Beard, A. (2021) Life's Work: An Interview with Tina Turner. *Harvard Business Review*, 1 February. Available at https://hbr.org/2021/01/lifes-work-an-interview-with-tina-turner (accessed 30 November 2022).
2. Ibid.
3. Petrusich, A. (2023) The Untouchable Tina Turner. *The New Yorker*, 25 May. Available at www.newyorker.com/culture/postscript/the-untouchable-tina-turner (accessed 1 June 2023).
4. Turner, I. and Turner, T. (1966) River Deep Mountain High. Los Angeles: Philles Records.

5 Turner, T. (1991) The Best. New York: Capitol/EMI.
6 Petrusich, The Untouchable Tina Turner.
7 Houston, E. (2019) Introverts vs Extrovert: A Look at the Spectrum and Psychology. *Positive Psychology*, 9 April. Available at https://positivepsychology.com/introversion-extroversion-spectrum/#:~:text=In%20social%20situations%2C%20extrovert%20and,to%20avoid%20social%20situations%20altogether (accessed 17 June 2023).
8 Hunt, E. (2023) What Personality Are You? How the Myers-Briggs Test Took Over the World. *The Guardian*, 30 August. Available at www.theguardian.com/lifeandstyle/2021/aug/30/myers-briggs-test-history-personality-types (accessed 17 June 2023).
9 Turner, I. and Turner, T. (1973) Nutbush City Limits. Inglewood: United Artists.
10 Turner, T. (1984) What's Love Got to Do With It? Los Angeles: Capitol.

WELL-BEING WIN 10

A Chapter by Tracey

Tom Daley and Creativity

[verb] The process of exploiting creativity and joy within the most mundane of tasks.

my curriculum sequencing was a bit dull, so I Tom Daley'd it?

WELL-BEING WIN 10: TOM DALEY AND CREATIVITY

Tom Daley OBE was born in Plymouth in 1994 – a little boy with big dreams who grew to richly earn his place in history as Britain's most decorated diver.[1] Considered a pioneer as an openly gay man in the often-heteronormative world of professional sport, Tom has redefined masculinity and success on his own terms and is now widely considered to be a national treasure.[2] Tom's talent and sparkle really teach us to work hard, to be resilient, to not give up and ultimately to be yourself. An idol for many young people in particular, he sets a precedent for how dedication and commitment can lead to greatness. He also teaches us to recognise that sometimes things go wrong, and it's what we do with these moments that truly counts.

Tom Daley's fame and influence transcended his discipline long ago. At the age of fourteen he became the youngest ever British Olympian at the Beijing Olympics. He has since gone on to become the first Team GB diver to win four Olympic medals.[3] A confirmed poster boy for Team GB in London 2012,[4] amid a cloud of media coverage Tom secured a bronze medal showing incredible focus in the face of unimaginable pressure and a media who wanted to report on every aspect of Tom's life – of which diving was just a part. However, having lost his father in 2011, he was open about the toll that grief played on his ability to focus and perform. There was a sense that Tom didn't quite deliver the goods in 2012 (despite winning a bronze medal); there was a feeling that he had been somehow over-hyped. However, the critics needn't worry as Tom's finest hour was yet to come …

It was in 2020 at the Tokyo Olympics where Tom's destiny as a record-breaking Olympian was realised. This saw the fruition of his dedication and the culmination of the work he began aged seven when he joined Plymouth Diving Club and the many sacrifices he'd made in the subsequent years. During these Olympics, Tom won two gold medals individually and with his diving partner Matty Lee. Tom credits this success to his mindset, having made a decision that diving didn't define him – thus alleviating some of the pressure he had felt in previous events.[5]

In 2013 Tom came out as gay, a move which can be considered pioneering in the world of professional sports. Having been bullied for his sexuality previously, Tom is now widely considered to be an LGBTQ role model, exemplified by his advocacy for same-sex parenting and awareness-raising work such as his 2021 BBC documentary 'Illegal to Be Me'.[6] He has also supported anti-bullying causes such as Childline and the NSPCC. By being at once vulnerable and unashamedly himself, Tom reminds us that neither success nor failure is permanent, and of the role creativity plays in personal growth.

Dive into Creativity

This entire chapter is inspired by the unforgettable image of Tom in his GB kit knitting at the Tokyo Olympics – something which (in his own words) 'kept him sane throughout this whole process'. (Approximately one million people are reported to have taken up knitting since this viral moment – dubbed the Tom Daley effect.)[7] Not only have studies proven that creativity can reduce stress and depression, it also affects brain function and improves neuroplasticity and cognitive function, and it's also utterly joyous – which we have already established is a well-being win within its own right!

So how can we do a Daley and tune out stress with creative endeavours? It's my experience that most teachers are naturally creative (perhaps even frustratedly so). In the DfE Working Lives of Teachers and Leaders Survey, 84% of respondents reported that they enjoy classroom teaching 'all/most of the time'.[8] We likely would agree that it's not the actual teaching (which is inherently creative in nature) which is detrimental to our well-being – but everything else which enables it. School leaders have a collective responsibility to respond to the issues of workload and well-being pragmatically – but also innovatively, creating opportunities to be creative wherever we can.

Create opportunities for creativity because:

▶ it promotes awe, wonder and joy!
▶ it leads to non-linear thinking which can result in higher levels of innovation and creative problem solving
▶ in terms of resourcing it's virtually free.

Win 1: 'Meditation made me better'[9]

Mindfulness can be defined as being intensely present within any given moment and being intentionally aware of our soundings. Mindfulness has emerged in recent years as a practice which boosts overall mental health and combats stress, with over a decade of research supporting its benefits.[10] Many schools explicitly deliver mindfulness to their learners; it's something that Tom does daily – and something we can all benefit from to be more present and focus our minds.

I completely understand that a mindful moment can feel like a luxury in the school day (many of us would opt for a cup of tea and a visit to the loo over a meditative moment). So how can we meaningfully implement mindful moments in a profession which is already time-starved?

Mindfulness can perhaps be best described as the antithesis of auto-pilot – an intentional and deliberate slowing down (physically and mentally) for us to re-centre and reflect. Though possibly counterintuitive to teachers because there is *so much to get done*, there are many easy ways to build mindfulness into everyday practice if we do a Tom and think creatively. At whole-school level offering mindfulness sessions/lessons or interventions for students is a great way for teachers to practise strategies in the

WELL-BEING WIN 10: TOM DALEY AND CREATIVITY

moment – building this into the school day as part of collective worship, form time, assembly or even as part of the school's enrichment programme will take no time away from the school day (nor from teachers themselves). Similarly, offering a mindful space at school during break and lunch time would similarly allow staff to benefit from a quiet(er) space in which to reflect.

Group mindfulness sessions could form part of staff inset or fulfil directed time – implemented successfully it could also reap huge rewards in terms of avoiding staff burnout which could later result in a reduction in staff absence. Mindfulness doesn't need to be a huge signposted event; it could simply be breathing exercises which can be completed very discreetly or (better yet) as role modelling for students.

Mindfulness benefits to keep in mind

- It boosts emotional regulation.
- It can distil or filter thoughts in order to narrow or clear the mind.
- It provides moments of stillness to reflect, to question, to clarify – opportunities which are few and far between on any day (let alone a school day!)
- It promotes compassion and empathy.
- It allows us to-reconnect and re-focus.

Daley/daily mindfulness which requires no resourcing

- Wiggle your toes; pay attention to what you can hear, see and feel.
- Focus on breathing – using slow and intentional breathing techniques.
- Set a daily intention – and bring yourself back to this as many times as needed.
- Out loud affirmations such as 'I've got this!' and 'My best is good enough' are beneficial for students as well as staff!

Win 2: 'Winning just feels like a natural extension of imagining that win'[11]

As we have already established we are all about the winning – so Tom's strategy of visualising success referenced in this quotation absolutely contributes towards enabling it. In terms of well-being, we should endeavour to be brave enough to envision a world in which we can be both succeeding and well – and also the tenacity and drive to bring that vision to life.

But vision can serve our well-being on a more practical level too: using visualisation strategies can boost concentration, help to regulate emotions and help us to strive for greater levels of efficacy. One way to use this is to imagine the most well version of yourself in as much detail as possible. How do you move? Walk? Stand? Talk? By regularly visualising them as vividly as you can, your brain will subconsciously start to find ways to bring your vision to life. This can also be helpful in terms of really identifying the gaps between your actual and ideal self which will allow you to consciously strive towards creating them.[12]

It could also be helpful for school leaders to envision the most successful school possible – one which has sensible working practices at its heart and allows staff and students to be the very best versions of themselves – and working backwards from that vision in order to identify key priorities and resources which could bring this to fruition. Imagining that which is perfect and comparing it to what we are actually working with can serve as a useful diagnostic on a whole range of school improvement priorities.

Creating a vision board for the academic year, ideal school, class or team can also be an extremely worthwhile exercise in the sense that it's a physical symbol of the goals you're working towards which could prove to be extremely motivating on a grey Monday morning in November when everyone is staying for parents' evening. Also, when embarking on any new task or project it's helpful to check in with the vision board to establish whether this work aligns with the broader vision.

Visualisation can:

▶ enable abstract ideas to become more tangible
▶ promote thinking 'out of the box'
▶ support risk taking and innovation
▶ boost innovation.

Visualisation can also be considered as a synonym for your mindset. If you choose and decide to have a positive day – you will. If you decide to really enjoy teaching Year 9 – you will. In the same way when on the cusp of a stressful high-stake situation like an inspection or interview, imagining it going perfectly well (in granular detail) will help to manifest that into a reality.

Win 3: 'Worry is a prayer for bad things to happen'[13]

We perhaps can all recognise that we all experience anxiety in some form during our lives – and especially within this great profession of ours. However, it feels important to point out that if you are experiencing new or worsening feelings of anxiety to please consult your GP. This well-being win is focused on worrying, without trivialising mental health or anxiety.

If you put the word 'amazing' into Google, it would generate lots of examples of things people consider to be amazing. If you put 'awful' into Google it would similarly generate examples of 'awful' – the brain is the same. In the same way that we tell our students the more they focus on the thing they find hard, the more of an obstacle it becomes. So Tom is right – the more we worry the worse the thing we're worrying about is likely to be.

Therefore, this well-being win is all about *creating* your reality – one in which we are not beset by worry and anxiety. Worrying is perhaps a by-product of caring; we have established that teachers care a great deal – but also that caring and being well are not mutually exclusive traits. We all know that worrying is detrimental, we know that worrying doesn't change outcomes but many of us will continue to worry regardless. Excessive worrying can increase cortisol levels in the body which can create the 'fight or flight' high-alert state – very much the opposite of what we're striving for.[14]

In the face of worry, Tom took control and channelled his anxiety into knitting – a masterclass in taking back control in a high-stakes accountability process. In some ways sitting on the bench at the Olympics could be considered akin to waiting for an interview/inspection/observation – though hopefully you don't do this in your swimwear(!) These are all instances which are pre-empting outcomes or the judgement of others, and in some ways may be worse than the thing itself.

Alternatives to worrying

- Make a list of your concerns and look at them objectively.
- Get physically active (outdoors if possible) and channel your anxiety into something which gets your heart pumping.
- Off-load – talking your worries through rationally and calmly can often lead you to finding solutions.
- Make a list of only the things you can influence and focus on them.

Anxiety that doesn't look like anxiety:

- Chasing perfection
- Intrusive thoughts
- Restlessness
- Difficulty in concentrating

The other aspect of this well-being win is the fact that Tom modelled a perfect solution to anxiety – and in doing so, Tom gifted the world an entire strategy to keep stress in check. The act of giving (in a way that doesn't 'take' anything from your overall well-being) is good for your mental health in itself, in the same way that modelling taking your own well-being/workload seriously will also empower others to do the same.

Other ways to allay worry

▶ Keep open lines of communication with parent/colleagues/students and your line manager.
▶ Use tools like planning documents/calendars/checklists to stay on top of tasks.
▶ Utilise your support network (in and out of school).

Ultimately, Tom Daley is an excellent example of how creativity can be the antithesis of pressure – by diverting our attention elsewhere, promoting mindfulness and fostering a sense of accomplishment. More than this, Tom is an example of how being proud of who you are (and aware of what we represent) is an absolute well-being win not to be underestimated.

Look out for the Tom Daley archetype in your school/trust network and watch how they:

▶ are acutely aware of their own well-being needs and how to allay them
▶ radiate joy and impact positively on the well-being of others
▶ can channel anxiety into creativity to the benefit of others.

Case Study

Miss S is a Senior Assistant Principal in a primary school within the Black Country who has done a Daley by seeking solace in her creative endeavours. Miss S is a naturally creative practitioner who reconciles the demands of her leadership role with spearheading an online book club on behalf of WomenEd – a project which feeds her well-being as well as enabling her to champion texts which have left an impact on her. The WomenEd book club not only amplifies marginalised voices (très Daley), but has proven to be a source of well-being magic for Miss S both professionally and personally – which feels every bit as valuable as an Olympic Gold medal.

WELL-BEING WIN 10: TOM DALEY AND CREATIVITY

As part of the first incarnation of the book club, Miss S's vision aligned with the core group for the book club to connect and communicate with like-minded professionals, initially to discuss the work of women in a genre which felt dominated by white male writers though the scope of the project has now transcended its original aim thanks to her creativity, commitment and values.

In the post-pandemic world, the book club gathered momentum – thanks in part to the rise of live streaming, which ensured the book club could be watched in real time. By now, Miss S was running the book club singlehandedly and had been given complete creative freedom – something she saw as a real privilege and honour, rather than additional workload.

Under Miss S's autonomous leadership, the book club thrived. Miss S's well-being was boosted by the opportunity to autonomously connect with readers and authors whose values aligned with her own, and the subsequent sense of community this facilitated. By enabling a safe space in which (most often, but not always) authors could discuss their lived experiences and texts – often with provocative and emotive perspectives – Miss S has found the book club to be an affirming and rewarding process which has brought her closer to her own values. The key to its success is authentic connections between individuals and platforms and honest, open communication. The book club has now grown organically into a credible forum which secures participation from relatively high-profile authors and texts.

Further creative opportunities have arisen to connect with key events such as International Women's Day and World Book Day and though these events require time, planning and commitment from others, the well-being output more than justifies the initial outlay. The thread that weaves all of the book clubs and subsequent events together is values which has reminded Miss S of the power of connection and collaboration and has ultimately served as first-rate CPD – not least of all because it has sparked considerable amounts of joyful professional curiosity. But the real well-being win for Miss S has been the sense of belonging and cohesion which has been a glorious by-product of her creativity.

Conversation Starters

Create Daley motivation for creativity with the following talking points

Can we take a step back and pause before we act?

Is there a different way to look at this?

If we had a magic wand, how would we want this to look?

Final Takeaway

There's no gold medal for struggling – so don't drown in your feelings, dive into something creative and you'll be awash with coping strategies.

Notes

1. Ferguson, D. (2023) Tom Daley Sets Sights on Paris Olympics after Confirming Diving Comeback. *The Guardian*, 20 July. Available at www.theguardian.com/sport/tomdaley (accessed 1 August 2023).
2. Ibid.
3. Daley, T. (2021) *Coming Up for Air*. HQ.
4. Mashiter, N. (2021) Tom Daley's Diving Career: From London Breakthrough to Tokyo Olympics Gold Medal Triumph. *The Independent*, 26 July. Available at www.independent.co.uk/sport/olympics/tom-daley-gold-medals-tokyo-diving-b1890625.html (accessed 1st August 2023).
5. Ferguson, Daley Sets Sights on Paris Olympics.
6. Hattenstone, S. (2022) Tom Daley on his LGBTQ+ Awakening. *The Guardian*, 6 August. Available at www.theguardian.com/lifeandstyle/2022/aug/06/tom-daley-lgbtq-awakening-gay-rights-british-commonwealth-documentary (accessed 6 August 2023).
7. Wood, Z. (2022) Tom Daley Effect Spurs Men to Take Up Knitting Amid Home Crafting Boom. *The Guardian*, 9 January. Available at www.theguardian.com/lifeandstyle/2022/jan/09/tom-daley-effect-spurs-men-to-take-up-knitting-amid-home-crafting-boom (accessed 19 August 2023).
8. Department for Education (2023) Working Lives of Teachers and Leaders Wave 1. Available at www.gov.uk/government/publications/working-lives-of-teachers-and-leaders-wave-1 (accessed 4 November 2023).
9. Lewis, O. (2019) Tom Daley: Meditation Can Help Me Win Diving World Title. *Telegraph*, 7 May. Available at www.telegraph.co.uk/olympics/2019/05/07/tom-daley-meditation-can-help-win-diving-world-title/ (accessed 19 August 2023).
10. NHS (2022) Mindfulness. Available at www.nhs.uk/mental-health/self-help/tips-and-support/mindfulness/ (accessed 20 August 2023).
11. Daley, *Coming Up for Air*.
12. Marson, G. (2021) The Benefits of Visualisation. *Dr Gia Marson Blog*, 21 July. Available at https://drgiamarson.com/the-benefits-of-visualization/ (accessed 20 August 2023).
13. Daley, *Coming Up for Air*.

CONCLUSION
A Chapter by Charlotte

> What have learnt and what impact could it make?

> What are the next steps in creating cultures and climates conducive to well-being?

DOI: 10.4324/9781003409113-13

CONCLUSION

So, what have we learned? Importantly, what can we pass on and what wisdom can we disseminate to others? How can we support colleagues and how can we help new teachers, as well as grow and protect a profession and vocation that is so valuable?

Some of the statistics within teaching do not paint a positive picture – 'teacher burn-out' being a common phrase embedded within education, teachers staying in the profession for an average of three years and then moving on to a different job entirely. Also, the cost-of-living crisis means that teacher strikes have been apparent throughout the country in the academic year 2022–23, due to feelings of unrest at rates of pay among a difficult financial time. Headlines reference the reasons as being 'the toxic mix of low pay and excessive workload'. At the time of writing, a gloomy picture permeates through the educational world, a grey image that we desperately need to inject some colour and joy back into …

Yet, it still remains a fantastic and rewarding career – biased as we may be! After teaching literally thousands of children between us, we can safely say that the impact we all as teachers, leaders and educationists generally can have on pupils everywhere is not to be underestimated. I love nothing more than seeing pupils years after they have left school, maybe even following them graduating from university. I love seeing pupils who have become successful, achieved their dreams and ambitions, and I feel even more maternal and bursting with pride when they tell me that they themselves have become teachers because of us (I'm not crying …) Most of all, I feel such a sense of pride when I can see the well-rounded young adult they have become and how the content of their character shines. This is *so* rewarding.

The foundations of teacher well-being for me are crucially relationships – the relationships between us and the young people in our care, relationships between ourselves and other colleagues, creating a sense of teamwork, togetherness, a collaborative culture, and the relationships between other stakeholders, whether this be families, governors and other professionals or agencies. Each are cornerstones in any workplace in my view, but particularly within schools. They help to build up the educational community and family, keeping it robust, stable and also better prepared and insulated from challenges that the school may be faced with, helping to future-proof the profession.

We spend a *lot* of hours at work and a lot of time dedicated to thinking and reflecting about work. The thought of not being happy or content in our roles is too much to bear. Compassion, empathy, dedication and teamwork are some of the values our icons within the chapters and, most of all, the real-life *teacher icons* epitomise. We can learn so much from all and writing this has taught us, the authors, such a lot collectively too.

Just imagine schools around the world built on such principles. Imagine the improved retention numbers and, overall, imagine the consistency that our young people and future generations would have in their education journey. Most importantly, just imagine the positive role models that would be helping to shape their futures! The well-being drive and shift would really be quite something to contend with.

What Are the Next Steps in Creating Cultures and Climates Conducive to Well-being?

Some (cynics!) may feel that all of these principles and, indeed, the concept of following in the footsteps of famous people could sound a little idealistic. I obviously disagree …

If you have not picked up anything from this book (first of all, do feel free to reread!) please, please do take away this: it is apparent that well-being and cultivating a culture and ethos of work–life balance lead to a more harmonious workplace, a happier school with staff and pupils that are full of contentment. This further leads to higher productivity levels and outcomes. Colleagues are much more likely to work with you if well-being is balanced and, most of all, if people are *happy* at work, the children are happy and the workplace achieves so much more! Even beyond results and league tables.

Some Basic Things That Can Have a Great Impact in Schools

You will notice that throughout the book there are some themes and common threads that are woven throughout several chapters. For example, we like to emphasise the importance of collaboration, teamwork, ambition and, above all, compassion. Being true to yourself and integrity are common values that also permeate throughout the book and I hope that you as readers can appreciate the links with well-being and most importantly use and apply the recommendations given.

We also ultimately wanted to emphasise the positive representation of protected characteristics. We are all unique and individual. As teachers, we may have received very similar training; our own educational pathways leading to our careers may be mirrored, but as *people* we are all uniquely and beautifully ourselves – thank goodness for this! The focus on race, gender, sexuality, religion, disability, marriage and family life throughout the book, included in both our celebrity biographies and also within our real-life case study examples, form what is ultimately a rather fabulous tapestry of individuality and an appreciation of this uniqueness. A *celebration* of these if you will. It is this celebration that needs to be spilled over into the workplace too, as each of us – our personality and characteristics – can contribute something different and help to develop ourselves, each other and the schools in which we work when inclusivity is not just simply acknowledged, but embedded.

We fully advocate teachers, leaders, everyone who works in education to support and encourage our children and young people to unapologetically be themselves, rather than live in the shadows of denial or repressed feelings. Teaching the future generation to have confidence and effervescence, love, care, compassion, grit and hard work are ingredients for happiness and well-being, but most of all, being wholeheartedly *you* is absolutely necessary and crucial to happiness and healthy minds in a complex world – and they don't come much more complex than the world of teaching.

So go forth and authentically share the well-being wins as far as you're able, look for the small scale wins and know that the bigger ones will follow. Treat well-being as something we can win, and feel emboldened to call out the time thievery or work for the sake of work. But most of all remember that a school's most valuable resource will always be its staff.

Afterword

To conclude, we'd like our case study icons to have the final word in terms of their ultimate tips for well-being.

Beyoncé AKA Mr R

High expectations and positive relationships can coexist – don't work for the sake of work and don't be afraid to call out time thievery when you see it because everyone's time is precious.

Robbie Williams AKA Mrs B

Having a child-centred approach in education is absolutely crucial. You will never go far wrong with this attitude. Being creative, resourceful and playing to strengths is also important within education.

Dame Kelly Holmes AKA Miss D

Always aim to tackle challenges with optimism, utmost professionalism and calmness, particularly within a pastoral role (as difficult as this can be at times). Resting and recuperation are also imperative to well-being and help us to tackle adversity and difficulties in a fast-paced job and, of course, it helps us to be better practitioners in the long run.

Professor Stephen Hawking AKA Mr D

Struggle and pressure are inevitable – allowing them to hold you back is not. In times of personal adversity, the routine and community offered by working within a school can be enormously motivational.

AFTERWORD

Taylor Swift AKA Mrs T

Never underestimate your instincts; there are competing directives in education, but ultimately staying true to your core values is key – not only to allay stress, but also to ensure you can sleep soundly at night. In the early years of my career I lost sleep wondering whether I was doing enough/too much for my students. If in doubt ask yourself what is in the best interests of your students and remember why you came into the profession.

Marcus Rashford AKA Mr B

Helping others and making a difference through reaching out in the wider community is great for well-being. Just ensure that you have effective tools to wind down and switch off – particularly when working in a safeguarding role.

Dolly Parton AKA Mrs KS

Do not waste time and ask before completing any task: 'will this help the children?' If no, then it is perfectly acceptable to question the intent. Time thievery is banned! Effective time management may also sometimes appear in the form of making some decisions that mean balance is restored, such as asking to reduce hours or looking at flexible/casual working if it helps your family life. Just stay true to you.

Joe Wicks AKA Mrs H

Positivity helps everything. A healthy mind, focusing on hope in dark situations, leads to success and a healthy mentality. Positivity radiates and helps everyone's well-being.

Tina Turner AKA Miss M

Do not dedicate any of your time and energy into worrying what others think of you. I guarantee that no one in the profession has time to deliberate over whether you are working too self-indulgently or holding your boundaries.

Tom Daley AKA Miss S

Your well-being will thrive when you are kept close to your values. Actively seek out the opportunities to re-affirm these and connect with others whose core values align with yours. Nourishing your well-being is the constant you should invest your energy in. Align your well-being with nurturing and living your values by seeking out connections that re-affirm and ground you – remind you of your why. Your why being much bigger than you and being part of something bigger – it's organic and something we have in abundance working in schools.

Index

adaptability 44, 45
Adverse Childhood Experiences xv
alter ego (persona), professional 15–16, 97
ambition 36, 64, 74, 75, 76, 86, 113
anxiety 2, 105–7
approachability 16
aspiration 36, 37, 73, 93
authentic self 15, 97
autonomy 18, 77; workload 2
availability 16

Beyoncé 11–17, 19, 115
big picture thinking 43, 44, 65
Black, White, Gold (Holmes) 33
boundaries: banishing guilt about 96; setting and honouring 55, 95–6, 97
burn out 75, 84, 104, 112

care/caring 106; self-care 13–14, 35, 36
change: getting on board with 44–5; inevitability of 44
change management xiv-xv
coaching 74; in-house 76; leadership 17–18, 98
collaboration 14–15, 24, 74–5, 113
communication 24, 38, 39, 56, 74
compassion 9, 24–5, 61–9, 112, 113; individual level 66; teacher case study 67–9; whole-school level 66
confidence 23, 26, 34

continuing professional development (CPD) 73, 74, 86
creativity 101–9, 115; conversation starters 108; as means of allaying worry/anxiety 105–7; mindfulness 103–4; teacher case study 107–8; visualisation 104–5
cultural capital 66
culture: collaborative 15; confident and self-assured 26; of effective feedback 27, 34, 36; of positivity 34
Cyrus, Miley 75

The Daily Mail 32–3
Daley, Tom 101–3, 106, 107, 117
Dame Kelly Holmes Trust 32
Day, C. 39
Department for Education 4; Schools' Financial Benchmarking website 29; *Working Lives of Teachers and Leaders* report 2
depression 2
diet/eating well 13, 84, 86
diversity 5
drains and radiators 95

eating well/diet 13, 84, 86
Education Endowment Foundation (EEF) 45; Report on Effective Professional Development 73; Teaching and Learning Toolkit 29

INDEX

email policy 56, 96
emotion, and practice, separating 97
emotional intelligence 62, 65–7
empathy 62, 65–7, 112
energy sources, understanding your 94
Energy Vampires 95
enrichment opportunities 26, 47
entertaining 23–4
Equality Act (2010) xv
exercise 13, 82–4, 86, 87
extra-curricular activities 26
extroversion/introversion preferences 93–4

feedback 36, 47; culture of effective 27, 34, 36; means of conveying 85; positive 34, 47, 85
fun, having 24, 27

Gordon, J., *The Power of Positive* 89
The Guardian 32
guidance 75–6
guilt, boundary 96
Gu, Q. 39

habits, healthy *see* healthy habits
Harris, Nadine xv
Hawking, Stephen 41–3, 44, 45, 46, 48, 115
Health and Safety Executive 2
healthy habits 11–19, 86; collaborating with others 14–15; conversation starters 18; cultivating a professional alter ego 15–16; habit stacking 13–14; modelling 16; self-care 13–14; teacher case study 17–18
help and support 75–6: accepting and giving 38, 39; asking for 26; phone line-based 97
Holmes, Dame Kelly 9, 31–3, 34, 36, 115
humour 23, 27, 46

iconic individuals, learning from 4–5
imposter syndrome 33–4, 74
improving not proving 45–6
inclusivity 5, 113

The Independent 63
integrity 89, 113
intelligence: as the ability to adapt 44, 45; emotional 62, 65–7
introversion/extroversion preferences 93–4

Joe Wicks: Facing My Childhood (documentary) 83–4
joy, promoting 46–8

kindness 68–9, 89
Kotter, John, *My Iceberg is Melting* xiv–xv

laughing at ourselves 23
laughter 46
leadership coaching 17–18, 98
learning 73; from mistakes 89; from others 89; openness to 89
listening 68
love 24, 96–7

Markle, Meghan 13
mental health xiii, xiv, 3, 8, 9, 28, 29, 35, 63, 69, 83–5, 97
mindfulness 103–4
mindset 105; performer's 26; transformation of 9
mistakes, learning from 89
Moodhovers 95
Mueller, David 52
Myers-Briggs personality test 93
My Iceberg is Melting (Kotter) xiv–xv

negative moments 85
'no', saying 55, 84

Ofsted 2; inspections 43
'open door' policy 27, 76, 86
openness 39, 74

Parton, Dolly 9, 71–3, 75, 116
pastoral care 34, 35, 36–7, 66, 75, 97, 115

INDEX

Patterson, James 72
performer's mindset 26
personas, professional 15–16, 97
phone line-based support packages 97
positive feedback 34, 47, 85
positivity 9, 33, 34, 81–90, 116; individual level 86; talking points 88–9; teacher case study 87–8; whole-school level 86
The Power of Positive (Gordon) 89
praise, giving and receiving 36, 74, 76
pressure 41–50, 115; and big picture thinking 43, 44; de-escalating high-pressure situations 43–4; teacher case study 48–9
pride in achievements 34–5
prioritising workload 53–4, 56, 95
professional development 73, 74, 86
protected characteristics xv, 4, 113
PSHE curriculum 66
pupil-centred approach 25–6

radiators and drains 95
Rashford, Marcus 9, 61–3, 64, 116
relationships, as foundation of teacher well-being 112
'resetting' 85
resilience 3, 9, 31–40, 53; individual level 36; talking points 38–9; teacher case study 37–8; whole-school level 36–7
resourcefulness 21–30, 115; talking points 28–9; teacher case study 27–8
resourcing 2
retention of teachers 8
rewards, visibility of 47

safeguarding children 43, 53, 57, 63, 67–8, 97, 116
school councils 26, 28
self-assurance 23, 26
self-awareness 91–100; conversation starters 99; introversion/ extroversion preferences 93–4; and managing tasks in school holidays 95–6; teacher case study 98; understanding own energy sources 94
self-belief 26, 34
self-care 13–14, 35, 36
self-discipline 13
self-evaluation 76
Shellard, Paul 42
sleep 13
'sleeping on it' 38, 39
star of the week nominations 47
strengths, knowing own and others' 24
stress 2
success: defining 35; differing perspectives on 36; encouraging 37; visualising 104, 105
support *see* help and support
survival, thriving versus 13
Swift, Taylor 51–3, 55, 57, 58, 116

Teacher Well-being at Work report (TES) 2
Teacher Well-being Index xiv
teamwork 63–4, 75, 112, 113
TES, *Teacher Well-being at Work* report 2
TES School Well–being Report 2023: UK 2
thriving, versus survival 13
time investment 29
time management 9, 71–9, 116; talking points 78–9; teacher case study 77–8
time thievery 18, 29, 114, 115, 116
toxic workplaces 74
transparency 27, 39, 74, 96
Turner, Tina 91–3, 97, 116

vision boards 105
visualisation 104–5

well-being 2–3; new found focus for 8–9; overcomplication of term 9; what it is 3–4; why it matters 3
Wicks, Joe 9, 81–4, 116
Wiliam, Dylan 45
Williams, Robbie 21–3, 24, 115

INDEX

words, power of 24, 85
Working Lives of Teachers and Leaders report (DfE) 2
work—life balance 8, 78, 87, 113
workload 2, 51–9; acceptable 2; audit 56; autonomy 2; boundary setting 55, 95–6; conversation starters 58; distributing 14; email policy 56, 96; nice ways to say no 55; prioritising 53–4, 56, 95; shake it off mantra 53–4; teacher case study 57–8; unnecessary 8; whole-school level 56
worry/anxiety 2, 105–7

For Product Safety Concerns and Information please contact our EU
representative GPSR@taylorandfrancis.com
Taylor & Francis Verlag GmbH, Kaufingerstraße 24, 80331 München, Germany

www.ingramcontent.com/pod-product-compliance
Lightning Source LLC
Chambersburg PA
CBHW080225170426
43192CB00015B/2757